PRAISE FOR *CAPITALIZING*

"The competitive, perfectionistic, or obsequious parts of people that they rely on to climb the corporate ladder do not necessarily serve them when there's chaos. At that point, they need to access and lead from their Self, an inner essence of qualities like calm, confidence, clarity and compassion. Until this wise and entertaining book, no one has told them how to do that. As Rob Kalwarowsky carefully documents, chaos can create toxic workplaces. To capitalize on chaos, Self-leadership is the answer. Self-leadership is contagious and brings out the Self in everyone. This book can help achieve that kind of transformation and I hope it is widely read."

—**DR. RICHARD SCHWARTZ,** world-renowned psychologist, inventor of Internal Family Systems, Founder of IFS Institute, author of 10+ books

"Rob Kalwarowsky doesn't just talk about transforming chaos—he *lives* it. As someone who has personally worked with Rob as my coach, I've experienced the power of his insights, his deep empathy, and his relentless commitment to helping others find clarity in the midst of uncertainty. His story isn't just inspiring—it's a roadmap. This book is for anyone who's ever questioned their place in a toxic work environment, battled their inner critic, or felt overwhelmed by the pressures of modern leadership. Rob's vulnerability, combined with his mastery of self-leadership and the human operating system, makes *Capitalizing on Chaos* both a powerful read and a transformational tool. If you're serious about becoming a more authentic, grounded, and courageous leader—start here."

—**CHARLI K. MATTHEWS,** Leadership Coach and CEO of Empowering Women in Industry

This book is a reminder that we all hold the answer to chaos within us. Rob Kalwarowsky's approach to leadership invites readers to rise above chaos, step into their authentic self, and inspire that same transformation in others.

Rob Kalwarowsky's work echoes a powerful truth—when we remember our worth, we no longer result to fear-driven behavior. This book is more than a guide to profiting on chaos and becoming a better leader; it's a call to honor ourselves and create workplaces where everyone can thrive."

—**MATT ZEMON**, CEO and Founder of Bernard, author of *Psychedelics for Everyone*

"In the grand theatre of business, where uncertainty often takes center stage, *Capitalizing on Chaos* doesn't flinch—it stands tall, with sleeves rolled up and a spark in its eye. This book is a *compass for courageous leaders*, a call to action for those who refuse to be defined by disruption.

What struck me most as I read was this: chaos isn't the enemy. In fact, it's the invitation. Rob Kalwarowsky doesn't merely suggest this—he *proves* it, through clear-eyed strategies, real-world examples, and a deep understanding of what it takes to lead when the rulebook is burning.

This is not a book of theories—it's a manual for momentum. It speaks to those of us who've lived through seismic change, those who know that the greatest legacies aren't born in comfort, but in crucibles. And it does something few business books manage to do: it blends execution with empathy, urgency with humanity.

As someone who has coached thousands through reinvention—doctors, CEOs, authors, visionaries—I know what it takes to lead through turbulence. This book *nails it*. It reminds us that the leaders who rise are the ones who see possibility where others see paralysis.

To every founder, executive, speaker, and changemaker reading this: If you're looking for a blueprint to not just *survive* chaos—but to *capitalize* on it—this belongs on your shelf. Right now.

Final word from Dr. Al: If you've ever asked, '*What now?*' in a moment of uncertainty—this book is your answer. Not just timely—transformational."

—DR. ALLEN LYCKA, author of The Secrets To Living A Fantastic Life,host of Live with the Famous Dr. Al

"It's time to rise above fear-driven leadership, especially if it's the voices inside your own head. Smart, funny, and brutally honest, Rob Kalwarowsky learned how to not just survive chaos but thrive; making you a better leader both inside and out. This is the go-to guide for executives to do the same."

—LAURA GASSNER OTTING, WSJ Best Selling Author of Wonderhell, Washington Post Best Selling Author of Limitless, TEDx Speaker with Over 2 million Views

"Every CEO needs this book. Uncertainty and chaos are everywhere but how you show up, as a leader in your organization, can be a source of clarity, calm and order. The journey of transformation begins with yourself, and the results are felt by everyone around you. If you want to change your company, and capitalize on chaos, start by changing yourself."

—CHASE DALTON, Founder and CEO, Silicon Signs

"The world is messy, unpredictable, and full of noise. But as a leader, your job is to cut through it—to bring clarity where there's confusion, calm where there's chaos. And it starts with you. If you want to see change in your company, don't wait for the storm to pass. Start by changing yourself, and you'll inspire everyone else to rise with you."

—ROBIN DANIELS, Chief Business Officer, Zensai, LinkedIn Top Voice

"In a world drowning in leadership jargon and surface-level quick fixes, Rob Kalwarowsky's book is a lifeline. With raw honesty, real-life experience, and deep coaching insight, Capitalizing on Chaos cuts through the noise and addresses the chaos where it truly lives—inside us."

—JOHN R. MILES, Host of the *Passion Struck®* podcast and author of *Passion Struck* and *You Matter, Luma*

"Rob Kalwarowsky gets to the heart of what real leadership takes in a chaotic world: clarity, courage, and self-awareness. Capitalizing on Chaos is a wake-up call for anyone who thinks you can lead others without first leading yourself."

—DAMON LEMBI, CEO, *Learnit,* Author of *The Learn-It-All Leader* and host of *The Learn-It-All Podcast*

"For anyone who's ever worked under a bad boss or is worried they might be one—this book is a powerful resource. At a time when employee engagement is low and uncertainty abounds, this book offers clarity, compassion, and insightful strategies anyone can adopt to become a great manager. Rob's wisdom helped me realize that my experiences are valid—and that I am more than the sum of my thoughts. Every manager should read this book."

—MAMIE KANFER-STEWART, Author of *Momentum: Creating Effective, Engaging and Enjoyable Meetings,* Host of *The Modern Manager Podcast*

"In a world where chaos is constant and AI is shaking things up, this book is a must-read for leaders ready to turn the mirror inward. Capitalizing on Chaos doesn't just challenge you—it dares you to lead yourself first. True growth? It's an inside job. Master your parts. Thrive."

—WESLEY EUGENE, CTO/CIO, renowned tech leader featured at Fast Company's Innovation Festival, Collision, and the TBM Conference

CAPITALIZING
ON
CHAOS

CAPITALIZING
ON CHAOS

THE EXECUTIVE'S GUIDE TO
SUCCEED IN DISRUPTION

ROB KALWAROWSKY

KALWAROWSKY CONSULTING SERVICES INC.
www.robkalwarowsky.com

Cover design by *the*BookDesigners
Interior design by Liz Schreiter

Paperback ISBN: 979-8-9925409-5-6
Ebook ISBN: 979-8-9925409-4-9

KCS

ACKNOWLEDGMENTS

This book would not have been possible without the love, support and expertise of the following people. Thank you so much for supporting and guiding me.

My Mom & Dad, my beautiful wife Mbalia, Ellis Kim, Belle Hanneman, Dr. Karthikeyan Ganapathy, Dr. Richard Schwartz, Sunny Strasburg LMFT, Dr. Dave Lovas, Chris Westfall and, the world's greatest Labradoodle, Winston.

CONTENTS

FOREWORD

By Solange Tuyishime Keita

Founder and CEO of Elevate International, UNICEF Ambassador,
and Miss Universe Canada Delegate

In a world where complexity has become the norm—where economic uncertainty, AI disruptions, political instability, and social unrest collide—chaos has become a defining element of our time. But within that chaos, I see not just fear or dysfunction. I see an urgent invitation. An opportunity. A call to return to something far more powerful than control: our shared humanity.

Leadership today must be more than a title or strategic output. It must be a sacred responsibility—a conscious commitment to elevate others while staying grounded in our own self-awareness. Rob Kalwarowsky understands this. In *Capitalizing on Chaos*, he doesn't offer surface-level tactics or recycled leadership clichés. He invites us into a deeper, more transformative conversation: one where we learn to lead from within.

As someone who has walked through war, rebuilt life as a refugee, and risen as a global voice for equity and healing, I know that true leadership is born not from ease, but from how we respond to adversity. The greatest leaders I have met—across boardrooms, refugee camps, and global stages—share one thing in common: they choose compassion over ego, curiosity over control, and presence over performance.

Rob's work speaks directly to this kind of leadership. He boldly dismantles toxic patterns we've normalized for too long—arrogance, gaslighting, passive aggression—and offers a research-driven roadmap back to emotionally intelligent, deeply human leadership. He dares us to believe that even amid chaos, we can lead with clarity, courage, and care.

In these pages, you'll find not only strategic tools but also a profound reconnection to what matters most: people. Teams are not numbers. Employees are not machines. We are humans first. And when we lead from that truth—when we see and support the people behind the performance—we ignite something far more powerful than productivity. We build cultures of trust, resilience, and belonging.

Let us remember: the success of any organization is not measured solely by its profits, but by the wellness, engagement, and dignity of its people. That is the kind of legacy we are called to create.

So, to every executive, leader, and changemaker holding this book—thank you. Thank you for daring to lead differently. For being willing to look inward. For understanding that when we lead with heart and intention, we do more than succeed in disruption—we create a world worth inheriting.

May this book guide you, challenge you, and strengthen the kind of leader the world needs now more than ever: one who leads not in spite of chaos, but because they have found their purpose within it.

With gratitude and hope,
Solange Tuyishime Keita
President and CEO of Elevate International

INTRODUCTION

> "Step into the fire of self-discovery. This fire will not burn you, it will only burn what you are not."
>
> —MOOJI, JAMAICAN SPIRITUAL TEACHER

I never could have predicted this."

My wife poked her head out of the kitchen. She wondered who I was talking to. Sitting in the living room, I was looking out the back patio, staring at the jungle. A thick grove of trees stared back at me, a dense mix of palm fronds, infinite leaves, and the occasional exotic bird. Outside the open patio door, just beyond the balcony, howler monkeys, sloths, and iguanas hid inside those trees. All around me were things I never could have predicted. And, for a long time, I never would have allowed them into my life.

I was a long way from Alberta, Canada.

At my feet, the world's greatest labradoodle was taking a nap. My beautiful wife smiled at me, and I smiled back. The breeze through the open windows felt perfect. The gratitude was overwhelming. At last, I had found it: my kind of chaos.

Chaos is unpredictable. Like life inside the jungle's ecosystem. Or the choices that led me to Costa Rica. The human imagination, it seems, is always fluctuating and shifting—just as our economy and geopolitical forces move all around us. Yet, from inside chaos comes... well, what exactly?

The answer may surprise you:

Everything.

The great French painter, Paul Cezanne, said that we live in a rainbow of chaos.

And he was right. But chaos doesn't always look like a rainbow.

I'm guessing you know what I mean. LinkedIn polls show that 64% of professionals feel overwhelmed by the rapid pace of workplace change. As a result, nearly 70% of workers are searching for more support and coaching than ever before. Technology is driving the chaos for many: the adoption of artificial intelligence (AI) has created uncertainty for nearly half of all workers, as many are worried about being left behind. Gallup polls show that employee engagement in the U.S. is at an 11-year low. How can companies find peak performance and accountability, inside these troubling statistics?

Harvard Business Review says that 75% of leadership training isn't effective because it doesn't address the leaders' mindset. Chaos rules the day.

It's time to find a new order. Time to discover how to learn and grow in uncertain times. Time to empower leaders (and team members) with a powerful understanding and a new capacity for turning change into progress.

THE GREAT TRAINING ROBBERY

Organizations are the victims of the Great Training Robbery. It's time to stop the madness and find new solutions to navigate the unknown (instead of being overwhelmed by it). Sorry, L&D pros, but this just in: training isn't working. Leaders have to see that, without higher-level coaching, technology initiatives are pure chaos. Inside the potential of AI lives deep uncertainty, fear, and frustration. Your company is being robbed of its greatest asset: the ability to collaborate, grow, and lead.

DEALING WITH CHAOS IS AN INSIDE JOB

Regardless of your title or station in life, you are your own boss.

You don't have to have a team of 10, 20, or 20,000 to be the boss. You are always in charge of yourself—and in charge of how you show up amid chaos. In the company of one, how's your engagement score?

How would you evaluate your personal leadership style? Are you kind, compassionate, and understanding... to yourself?

I wasn't.

I had built my life around what looked like certainty. I had embraced a kind of personal and professional success that, from the outside, looked like I had things figured out.

But on the inside? It was pure chaos.

I wrestled with constant depression. Suicidal ideation. Corporate frustration. My boss was a nightmare, even though it looked like I was living the dream. What was wrong with me?

Inside economic shifts, geopolitical maneuvers, unpredictable leadership choices, and twisting employment markets, it's easy to see chaos as something that's pervasive. Uncontrollable. Overwhelming.

But consider how growth comes from chaos, not order—and you will be stepping into the premise of this book. Because, at its heart, this book is about growth. Ultimately, this book will provide you with guidance so that you can share new insights with others: your team, your family, and most importantly, yourself.

We work hard to predict our lives, our meetings, our social calendars, and our key performance indicators. However, despite our search, uncertainty still exists.

Uncertainty is all around us. From heartbeat irregularities to indigestion, weather patterns to thought patterns, we exist inside complex and often unpredictable systems and impulses.

Does this fact give you pause? Concern? Heart palpitations?

Looking in the direction of personal and organizational growth, this book is designed to provide you with a sense of understanding within the uncertainty. An understanding of how to not only function during times of chaos, but also how to thrive despite it. To learn new pathways towards Self-leadership, so that you can improve your career and your company—and be of greater value to the people that matter most to you. To discover what it really means to get out of your own way, redefining self-acceptance to create a new level of performance. You can find some order, and some agency, inside of change and disruption—and there's never been a more important need for this level of understanding.

There are many ways of looking at chaos and seeing unpredictable patterns. The unpredictable nature of fire, for example, is part of the unpredictable nature of (wait for it) nature. Instead of looking at fractals, avalanches, weather patterns, fluid dynamics, population growth, and heartbeats (all examples of unpredictable and often chaotic systems), this book looks at the human operating system. In other words, the way that you experience and adapt to the level of uncertainty that we call chaos. For the purposes of this book, the place where we experience chaos is not in observing nature—but inside the experience of our human nature.

Circumstances and situations are always filled with change. Always. Fortunately, human beings are always filled with resilience. The challenge is: accessing our true nature inside of the unexpected. This book will show you how to see (and experience) chaos in a new way—a way that can help bring you back to your greatest strengths. Because chaos is something that we all access via our experience. And sometimes, that chaos is created for us by others—but always experienced inside of ourselves.

Are you ready to find a new experience within puzzling behaviors? Let's go to the source of the chaos and discover a new way around the self-destructive self-talk. It's time to handle perplexing and chaotic leadership choices, inside your organization (and inside of yourself). Inside our human nature, we find the chaos that needs some order.

Chaos is not a theory; it is a reality. And I am grateful for it—because it was chaos that brought me to Costa Rica. Chaos that led me to write this book. And chaos that is creating the world around us. I no longer fear the things that support me, because I understand who I am within this unpredictable ecosystem of life.

You're here to find some order inside yourself. And inside your business. That means identifying and addressing the real source of chaos at an experiential level. That way, you can see new ways of showing up inside an unpredictable world. And you can help team members (and team leaders) to access the behaviors that drive growth, regardless of market conditions.

> *Chaos is rejecting all you have learned.*
> *Chaos is being yourself.*
>
> —EMIL CIORAN, CZECH PHILOSOPHER AND AUTHOR

Before the pandemic, my wife and I had escaped from the snows of Alberta to attend a friend's wedding in Hawaii. I remember it like it was yesterday. We were walking by the ocean. I turned to her and said, "You know, I always dreamed of living on the beach," I told her. "Like those guys."

Six feet away, on our left, we saw an old-style Volkswagen camper van, with patches of rust and sand dotting its faded blue exterior. The side door of the van was open. Two suntanned dudes were selling trinkets and souvenirs underneath a yellow awning. The guys were shirtless and smiling. Talking with tourists, it wouldn't be long before they were back in the waves and doing something else that they loved.

My wife laughed at me when I said, "I would love to do that!"

"What do you mean?" she said. "Sell stuff out of a van?

I loved the idea of living on a beach. I loved the idea of freedom.

The beach sure seemed nice. But the uncertainty! How could I… how would I… who would I have to be, to find that level of personal and professional freedom? First of all, I would have to be independently wealthy, I reasoned. That way, I could "follow my bliss" right off a cliff, destroying my career and my finances without any real damage! Ha!

A part of me would never let that happen. A part of me wouldn't let me anywhere near a ridiculous idea like living on a beach. Living on a beach? Absurd! I could never embrace what I knew, deep down, was the real Rob—no way! Ridiculous! How could I be so vain, so brash, so foolish, as to be… myself?

But four years later, I had come to terms with that part of me that was saying "no."

Cut to my wife and me moving to Costa Rica.

A country I had never visited. And yet, here we are.

By the way, I don't live in a van, and I don't live on a beach. But I found the freedom that I saw on those surfers' faces. I found the courage to face the chaos.

And you can, too.

You don't have to quit your job or move to a foreign country in order to step into your true self. Inside chaos—the uncertainty that surrounds us all—is opportunity. The key to personal and professional growth is to give yourself permission to pursue it. And, by extension, coaching your organization to embrace it.

Self-leadership is the first step.

Between choosing a new path or choosing to show up differently inside the same one, we find a new order. Leadership—and leadership training—takes on a whole new meaning, as coaching comes into the conversation. Notice that we are always able to control our own actions—and our responses—to situations. So why is it that we so often choose to limit ourselves, finding reasons to suffer instead of succeed?

Invention does not consist in creating out of a void, but out of chaos.

— MARY SHELLEY, AUTHOR OF FRANKENSTEIN

This book is about finding new reasons to navigate chaos in a new way. In a world of increasing complexity and uncertainty, where artificial intelligence is changing the way we live and work, the unknown can seem overwhelming. Believe me, I've been there—I know what overwhelm feels like. The good news is that overwhelm doesn't have to win. You can still find your way back to yourself and to new levels of understanding, effectiveness, and collaboration inside this book.

This book is filled with exercises as well, so that you can not only create new habits but implement new behaviors. Look for "Breakdown to Breakthrough" as a resource inside each chapter—with action steps that you (and your organization) can take on a journey to new habits, increased awareness, and greater accountability.

Making better decisions, having less anxiety, relieving stress: these are just a few of the personal milestones along the journey. For your organization, a culture of inclusive leadership and greater understanding is the result. Improved communication, greater collaboration, and a removal of toxic behavior all add up to greater retention and increased engagement—inside any set of chaotic circumstances. Ultimately, from chaos comes greater growth and efficiency for the organization as a whole—if you understand how to access it.

The journey begins with self-awareness, and an open mind. As your coach, I will help you to see things in a new way, so that you can do things in a new way. And if you're wondering if I'm talking about you as a person, or your entire organization, the answer is yes. What's good for you is good for your team.

Control what you can control, inside of chaos. Step towards the person you know you can be—and your team will feel the difference. And remember, you don't have to go it alone. Picking up this book, you've already taken the first step. And I'm here to help you every step of the way.

If you are struggling with change, working for someone that doesn't understand you, and you're wondering if this is all there is, please remember: there's always more. Possibilities always exist. Growth is waiting for you.

Surrounded by idiots, bounced around by policies you didn't ask for, blanketed by the choices of others, you always have the ability to choose how you respond.

Because capitalizing on chaos is an inside job. Creating growth and innovation inside an organization happens one person at a time. Overcoming poor leadership, identifying new strategies, and embracing change: it starts on the inside. This book will show you where to begin, as we take a look at the destructive leadership behaviors that are ruining careers and robbing organizations of efficiency.

Finding order inside the external chaos, we recognize that bad behavior isn't just something reserved for others. We all have the capacity for self-sabotage via ineffective behavior. But the good news is that it doesn't have to be like this.

Based on years of study, as well as the work of internationally recognized scientists and psychologists, you will discover new insights into the human operating system. I'll share with you my own personal journey, from working with demonic bosses and toxic leaders, battling through depression, and discovering what's waiting for all of us, in the middle of chaos: growth.

CHAPTER 1

THE COST OF CHAOS

"The greatest of empires, is the empire over one's self."

"Disorder will ruin the greatest empire."

—PUBLIUS SYRUS, LATIN WRITER, 85–43 BC

I was coaching a water polo practice, leading my team through some difficult and challenging drills. In the heat of the moment, with everyone swimming furiously, my star player jumped out of the pool. What?!?

I had played water polo for MIT in college. Before college, I had played for the Canadian Junior National Team competing on a global stage. As you can imagine, my approach to coaching was as intense as the games I had played. There was no way my best guy was getting out of the pool—what kind of chaos was this?

My eyes nearly popped out of my head. I saw my most talented athlete just give up on himself, and on his team! As I walked towards him, fast—stepping across the concrete, I planned my verbal assault—I was furious! Still six steps away, I saw him reach into his gym bag.

He pulled out a syringe.

He took his insulin shot.

In an instant, a new understanding showed up for me.

Understanding, like insulin to a diabetic, was exactly what I needed at that moment.

Understanding and awareness kept me from being a complete and utter asshole.

And, by extension, that understanding helped the player to get back in the game.

Maybe you're wondering if the journey through chaos is one of awareness?

Trust your instincts, my friend. Let's be aware that the word "chaos" is a way to categorize something. In our effort to explain behavior and situations that don't make sense, we attach a label. And sometimes that label doesn't help us to define much of anything, other than the boundaries of our frustration, anger, and lack of knowledge.

After all, sometimes chaos is a good thing. Chaos can be an opportunity to shake things up—and turn things around. Chaos can force us to new levels of resourcefulness and teach us what we are made of. Chaos can be a driver for learning new skills (such as working with AI, for example), or for moving to another city, or for moving out of a bad relationship. Chaos can be a catalyst. But when a catalyst is introduced, if you remember your chemistry, something new comes from the chemical reaction. Are you ready to be changed by chaos, even if the outcome is unpredictable?

Unpredictable leadership is often the source of unwanted chaos, and I've suffered needlessly because of it.

I was working under the world's greatest micromanager. A champion of small ball for one and all, he wanted to dive into the details on every assignment. Under the disguise of caring and concern, he was stealing my ability to do what I had been hired to do. Have you been there?

The world champion micromanager, let's call him Zeke, asked me to do a report comparing two products from different vendors. To keep it simple, I'll call them Vendor A & B.

The problem was that Vendor A's products were having a ton of problems with manufacturer defects. Within a short amount of time, Vendor A's gear would break and need to be repaired. In addition, their products that were already installed were being warranty-repaired for defects. Their new products didn't last, so we had no long term data. There was no track record to rely on in an evaluation.

As an MIT engineer, working for a mining company, performance and metrics mattered to me. Vendor B had the better performance and the data to prove it. Their products were working for a long time (10+ years) and were operating normally. Guess who I liked better?

I recommended the superior solution: Vendor B.

I smiled as I hit "Send," transmitting my report to Zeke.

Just 73 seconds later, I got an immediate and unexpected reaction from my boss. He popped out of his office and marched towards me in much the same way that I had stomped towards my top player on the water polo team.

He was agitated. He talked as he walked, half-shouting from across the office: "Rob! Can you redo the report?" My colleagues stopped the scroll. They turned away from their workstations in shock. Some even stood up in their cubicles, just to see who was playing the role of Captain Chaos today.

In the blink of an eye, Zeke was standing at my desk.

It was British Columbia, Canada, in February. But Zeke was sweating.

The report was solid, the research on point. What was missing, I wondered?

"What if we removed the defect data, then what would we get?" he said. "Can you cut the data in a different way?" he pleaded.

He paced back and forth around my desk, looking at the floor as if he had dropped something.

I told him I would do what he asked. I spent more time making various graphs.

Ultimately, vendor B was always superior to A. The math didn't lie. I showed all of the graphs to Zeke, to see which ones he wanted to use.

None. None of them were good enough.

Here's the fun part. The next day, Zeke came to my desk and stood behind me.

He narrated what he wanted the executive summary to say, word-for-word, while I typed it in. How fun is that?!

Was I a highly-paid engineer with an MIT education, or a typist?

He completely fabricated the result and the conclusions in the report, to say what he knew the Vice President wanted to hear. When he was done, we sent the report to the VP.

You can probably imagine what I was thinking:

> "Why did you hire me when you just wanted someone
> to make up the results that you want to share? Why don't
> you just write the report yourself?"

The over-the-shoulder maneuver felt like an attack. Like I was a puppet. Not a person. My work and my character were dismissed. I became both a tool and a fool for my boss, as chaos seemed to color my world.

Then I realized why I was here. I was the middleman—the human shield for a business decision that might come back to haunt me. But not my boss, because Zeke was technically "not involved."

"You're going to lie to your boss and put my name on the report," I thought to myself. As I began to understand what was going on, things didn't look quite so chaotic. They were becoming painfully predictable.

A few days later, Zeke came back to twist the knife. Part of being the world's greatest micromanager means that you have to smile while you twist it in. And he did his job.

"Rob, the VP loved your report. Great work!" His smile was so wide he looked like a six-year-old seeing an Xbox for the first time.

He was proud to tell me that the VP liked "my" report.

For me, the recognition was a slap in the face. I didn't write the report. He was attributing my name to a lie.

I definitely don't condone deliberately manipulating data to lie to your boss' boss. In fact, this maneuver was completely contrary to what I reported—and to who I am.

This incident is a demonstration of how internal chaos controls our leadership. Unpredictable inputs led to uncertain outputs—even when I was able to produce, I was reduced from what I knew I was truly capable of delivering. If we let chaos control us, we destroy our people's ability to be at their best. That's what happened to me. The world's greatest micromanager was clearly in fear (for his job, for his boss's favor, for whatever). That fear was pushed onto me. At the time, I didn't understand what was going on, and that's why it felt like I was drowning in chaos.

I don't know about you, but toxic leadership doesn't work for me. Today, toxic culture is driving people to quit, crushing employee engagement scores, and robbing companies of both efficiencies and new revenues. If retention matters to your organization, consider how to train for it—making your teams "leadership proof" via guidance on ownership, Self-leadership, and accountability.

Today, toxic leaders are doing even more harm to organizations than ever before, creating environments of mental anguish instead of psychological safety. That's why it's vital to explore how to help employees deal with toxic leadership, as a foundational element of capitalizing on chaos.

And as more and more organizations turn to self-directed work teams, the ability to self-regulate and innovate has become more necessary than ever before.

This little exercise with Zeke violated everything that I value in life. Things like honesty. Integrity. And doing a good job. My values and my actions were in conflict.

The world champion micromanager had won this round. But the battle was not over.

Maybe you're wondering, "Rob, why didn't you just quit?"

First of all, quitting isn't always the solution. It's naïve to assume that another job is just a click away. It's not.

There are bills, obligations, and commitments to consider. The decision to quit isn't like turning off a light switch.

And change, at the time, wasn't a switch I could make so easily.

When quitting is a permanent solution to a temporary problem, it's not a good idea. I felt a sense of chaos and frustration. But I wasn't ready to make an irreversible decision to leave.

Plus, it's been said that "Everywhere you go, there you are." Sometimes, leaving is the right thing to do, even if you don't have your next move lined up. But the real challenge with Zeke wasn't my courage around quitting. There was something deeper going on.

I was unable to choose to leave my job because of the chaos in my own mind.

My boss was so self-unaware to the point that it was destroying my mental health. My mindset was the thing that had to change—and eventually, it did. As a result, I was able to move on in my career and in my life. But not before a lot of self-reflection—plus a concentrated dedication to coaching, personal performance, and self-worth.

Here's the real challenge: when toxic leadership created chaos for me, instead of seeing other options and other possibilities, I saw myself as the problem.

I know something now that I didn't know then.

I'm not the problem. I'm the solution.

And so are you.

I've coached hundreds of executives, entrepreneurs, world-class athletes, media personalities, and global celebrities. Not only that, but I've had the opportunity to work with some of the greatest coaches in the world, in both athletics and business. My personal journey of self-discovery, combined with a dedication to coaching principles, is designed to help you change your behaviors—and change your results—no matter what kind of chaos you are facing right now.

Because I know that progress is always possible when we begin with an open mind. Where your journey starts is never where it ends—believe me, I know.

Originally from Ottawa, Ontario, Canada, I went to MIT and played on the water polo team, where I was a three-time Academic All-American. I played on the Canadian Junior National Water Polo Team, and worked in industry, as an engineer and consultant for ten years—mostly in Alberta and British Columbia. I've spoken internationally on TEDx stages, and I currently work in executive coaching & professional speaking—helping people just like you to create greater ease, confidence, and impact. I'm on a mission to turn chaos into opportunity and to change companies from the inside out.

Today, I'm grateful for Zeke because his lack of character helped me to redefine my own. The cost of chaos, for an organization, doesn't have to affect your bottom line results. No matter what you're facing at work, or who you're facing it with, remember that chaos is a temporary circumstance. Often it's a simple misunderstanding—a scary label, misapplied to a situation, when we can't see other options. The cost of the misunderstanding can be significant, but there is reward in a new perspective on chaos.

A micromanager boss doesn't have to define you, your values, or your worth. And you don't have to be a bad boss to yourself, telling yourself lies and expecting to find the truth. I'm talking about lies like, "You are worthless." Or that you don't matter. That you are the error that needs to be corrected. That your work, effort, and skills are invisible. None of these thoughts is true.

Imposter syndrome is a dangerous game because it's a game where no one wins. Chaos is built on uncertainty. When we live inside a lie of the mind, we can't respond to what really needs our attention. Chaos can be applied to many situations and circumstances. But ultimately, "chaos" is a label that we apply to the unpredictable nature of life. When uncertainty goes beyond a certain threshold, which varies on an individual basis, we experience doubts, fears, control issues, and the entire gauntlet of triggered negative emotions. We can't respond to what is happening because we are so far gone into our heads and our own stories.

But given that no one can predict the future, chaos (change) is a constant. How do we function when chaos is all around us? When people don't support us? When changes unexpectedly hit us?

The first step is to remember the difference between a label for uncertainty (chaos) and what it is that you do know. You know that you are capable. You know that you are resourceful. You know that you have many tools (including AI) at your disposal. And you know that uncertainty and discomfort don't have to go together. You can be uncertain about something, and you don't have to suffer. Or did you forget that?

Clarity is the first step. Especially when it comes to identifying (and dealing with) chaotic and toxic leaders.

There's a bigger game on offer here—if you're willing to play. A game that will impact the way that you show up for yourself, your team, and your organization. Inside this game, you turn chaos into a competitive advantage. Ready to play?

CHAPTER 2

BEYOND EMOTIONAL INTELLIGENCE

> *"Progress is impossible without change, and those who cannot change their minds cannot change anything."*
>
> —GEORGE BERNARD SHAW, NOBEL PRIZE-WINNING AUTHOR AND PLAYWRIGHT

> *"Emotions are not our enemy; they are messengers. But like any messenger in a chaotic environment, their signals can sometimes feel garbled and urgent, demanding our immediate, often unthinking, attention."*
>
> —BRENÉ BROWN, TED SPEAKER, AUTHOR OF DARING GREATLY, AND RESEARCH PROFESSOR AT THE UNIVERSITY OF HOUSTON

You know that feeling—when you get cut off in traffic by some huge, lifted neon orange truck and you are stunned as the clown driving this enormous machine flips you off like it's your fault that you were taking up space in his lane? And you honk and curse, but you're thinking of how you would like to get a ladder, climb 16 feet up into the cab of the truck, and punch that guy in the throat?

Or is that just me?

How about that time when you got the email that your largest client just backed out of a deal? I've been there, and it doesn't feel great.

Have you ever had someone bring you news or maybe just a sideways glance that made you… furious?

Turns out, I'm not describing a personal anger management issue. I'm describing human nature.

We all have the capacity for anger inside of us. We all have a part of us that is a "hothead"—rushing forward when we have been wronged, slighted, neglected, or ignored. Sometimes, it's as if a part of me shows up, coming to my defense, ready to fight for what's right, and leading me to think of elaborate revenge scenarios inside the chaos that the world has given me. It's like that time at water polo practice, where I was ready to argue and defend and scold and holler and… guess what? None of that was needed. That aggravated part of me needed to take a rest—and, luckily, it did.

When we act out of character, overrun with emotion, we say things like, "I didn't recognize that part of myself!" You know what I mean?

We have all been there: in situations where we care so much, or fear so much, or need so much, that a part of ourselves just seems to take over. Notice that we all contain many parts. The poet, Walt Whitman, said, "I am large. I contain multitudes." Indeed, everyone does.

Our very existence is multi-faceted. We can find inside ourselves rage, yearnings, joy, sensitivity, shame—the entire gamut of human emotions is on tap. Not only do we have the capacity to experience fear, jealousy, elation, and obsession, but we have all experienced "giving in" to these parts of ourselves.

When we feel endangered, or ignored, or triggered in some other way, it's as if a part of us takes over. A part of our personality comes forward to address a perceived threat or respond to a remembered trauma. Unexpected and chaotic events—a sudden illness, the loss of a loved one, being passed over for a promotion, getting cut off in traffic—can make it seem like life is crashing all around us. Or, on the other end of the spectrum, we find ourselves incredibly determined, competitive, and ambitious—driven by a sense of lack that creates high achievement. We strive to reach a goal and then, once that goal is reached, we find ourselves still striving. We feel a never-ending sense of "you are not enough." We see the world as an unfinished work (even when the work is done).

Can you relate? Have you ever found yourself unable to take the win, enjoy the victory, step back, and celebrate the little things in life, because you had to "get back to the grind?" It's a feeling of perpetual imposter syndrome, always trying to fill your life with something that's missing, but you're not always sure what it is. Listen, I've been there—and if you're there now, inside that chaos, I just want to say: I see you.

The crash from these emotional experiences can be described as burnout, but there are other words as well, pointing to the chaos in our lives—the chaos inside ourselves.

Right now, there might be a part of you that's skeptical of where this chapter is headed. But, as you find with most chapters in this book, it's always headed back to you. And, in this case, back to the parts of you. The parts that protect, the parts that put out fires, the parts that drive and manage the accomplishments in your life. Inside each of us, every human being, we find these parts.

That's according to my colleague and fellow author, Dr. Dick Schwartz. Dr. Schwartz is a Chicago-based therapist who holds a Ph.D. in marriage and family therapy from Purdue University. In the 1980s, Dr. Schwartz developed an innovative approach to psychotherapy called IFS (Internal Family Systems). While this book isn't about therapy, there are some powerful lessons to be learned from inside the IFS framework.

If you are struggling in your life, your relationships, and your work, you can't perform at your best. You can't think clearly or creatively. When you are stuck inside chaos, struggling to show up, you've got to wonder: what's holding you back? Where is this chaos coming from?

When your impact and your effectiveness isn't a question of knowledge (you know how to do your job, right?) we have to take a fresh look at how to navigate the internal chaos inside ourselves. And, from there, we discover how to enable what your organization and your business really needs: growth.

Growth happens when people show up, for themselves and for the organization, with clarity amid chaos. If you don't have that clarity right now, you are not alone. And you are in the right place—because the answers you seek are inside of you. Inside your organization. Even inside the chaos. You just have to know where to look.

When I faced chaos inside myself, I turned to science. And when I found myself confused by the behavior of others, I turned to science once again. Turns out that discovering what's best for yourself is a great way to find out what's best for your business. And that's what IFS can help us to discover.

We all possess various parts to our personality. In his book, *No Bad Parts*, Schwartz explains it like this: "Remembering a time when you faced a dilemma, it's likely you heard one part saying, 'Go for it!' and another saying, 'Don't you dare!'" (Remember my walk on the beach in Hawaii? It was like two parts of me were fighting —one part seeking freedom, the other seeking security).

Dr. Schwartz takes conflicted thoughts and adds a new level of understanding. In these times of internal chaos, he says, "We don't pay attention to the inner players behind the debate. IFS helps you to not only pay attention to them [those parts] but also to become the active internal leader that your system of parts needs."

Could it be that chaos—or our experience of the world as uncertain, disorienting, and disturbing—is coming from one (or more) parts of our personality? And, if so, how can we come to understand these parts, how they work together, and how we might be wired (inside the human operating system) to perform at peak levels? Could a deeper understanding of parts help us to create a greater whole—not just on an individual level, but on an organizational level as well? What if you could become the "internal leader" that your system of parts needs, as Schwartz suggests? Would that discovery make you a better leader for your organization as well?

Ultimately, this is a book about leadership and organizational growth. It isn't a book about therapy. Dr. Schwartz has already written that book. This book is about finding a way to bring order to chaos, plain and simple, and capitalize on the human operating system.

I know from my own personal experience that the harder we try to get control of our emotions and thoughts, the stronger they become. It's as if the parts inside of us resist being shamed ("I shouldn't feel this way!") or exiled. Self-discipline and strength of will are great, but they're not sustainable when it comes to suppressing emotions. Try it sometime. Don't think of birthday cake, for example. How's it going so far? Thoughts come and go, and our emotions often follow suit.

Trying to control your thoughts and emotions is a fool's errand: unsustainable and unhealthy. Try to control your emotional state when you go to the funeral of a loved one who has passed away. Can you stop the grief? Why are you trying to suppress what you feel when you have to say goodbye to someone you love?

They say that grief is love persevering. To stop the grief, truly, you have to stop the way that you feel for that person. You have to abandon your memories, deny your feelings, suppress the truth... Does any of that sound healthy? The fact is, you can't stop that unstoppable force: the power of the human mind. Thoughts and feelings come and go, like the wind or the weather. When you see storm clouds, do you grab some rope so that you can somehow tie down the sky? No, that's ridiculous.

You accept that it's going to rain. And you reach for your umbrella.

Sometimes the most intelligent thing you can do is to accept what is. Acceptance goes hand in hand with understanding, as the first step to capitalizing on chaos. Turns out, you don't need mind control to go beyond emotional intelligence—and discover a new way to show up in your life. Just as you would accept that grief is a part of life, and rain is a part of the weather, we have many parts inside of ourselves.

There are parts of us that seem unbridled and untamed. These parts take over, in certain situations, in an effort to help—and yet, the end result is often a mountain of chaos, confusion, pain, and struggle. Situations get worse, not better—and I wanted to know why.

I had to understand what these parts were. I had to know how to work within this system that my friend had identified inside of IFS—as well as making my own discoveries along the way. I knew the pain that these parts were creating chaos for me—forcing over-reactions and harmful choices when that was the last thing my life (and my career) needed. Could I learn to turn these parts into a force for good, not just a cauldron of chaos? Somehow, I had to learn to accept myself—all of myself—but that wasn't where my journey began.

I knew how to do my job, so what the hell was wrong with me? (That was a part of me talking, but I didn't have the capacity to turn down the noise. I couldn't move from chaos to contribution!) In my career, I had the skills, the talent, and the attitude for success. But I was miserable, suffering, and struggling. Why? The gap wasn't a knowledge gap. It was a gap in understanding around how people really work. More importantly, how *I* worked. When I understood the inside, the outside transformed. Because I was able to tap into new knowledge around the human operating system. And now, that knowledge is what I share with my clients—as a coach.

HOW COACHING IS DIFFERENT THAN THERAPY

Carol Kauffman is a psychologist at Harvard Medical School, and she's also the Founder and Executive Director of the Institute of Coaching at the school. In an interview with *Forbes*, she explains that there are a number of mental illnesses and conditions (like clinical depression, for example) that require medical attention—and therapy is part of that treatment process. But coaching is different, she says.

"In therapy, you follow the trail of tears," she explains, referring to healing the traumas and challenges of the past. "In coaching, you follow the trail of dreams."

You're here to learn what's best for your business. To discover new ways of reaching your goals—and creating that trail of dreams. My focus here isn't on revisiting the past, but on creating the future. Here's how she explains the difference further:

> "There are two houses," Dr. Kauffman says, "for coaching and therapy. In each house, there are rooms that are similar." She's referring to the kinds of questions and probing that exist in each conversation. As a therapist and a coach, her viewpoint is multi-faceted. "You have to honor the house you're in," she says. In coaching, it's important to remember what the conversation is not. "It's not 'I know more than you and my job is to install that information into you'. Coaching is helping people to see what they do not know that they know." In other words, helping clients (or team members) to find their own answers. Coaching concentrates on sharing and revealing insights, opening up new possibilities (instead of resolving past trauma).

Let's set our sights on creating new pathways: new dreams and new growth, even when it looks like there's chaos all around us. Coaching provides a way for you to see things in a new way, and share things in a new way, so that your entire organization can do things in a new way. After all, growth is what every business wants. And personal growth is what every person needs.

In the next chapter, we are going to take a deeper look at the science behind particular types of behavior. We will look at six examples of destructive leadership—the kind of approach that creates chaos inside organizations and struggles inside teams. As you meet The Destructive Six (that's what I call these examples of leadership), remember that these scientifically identified patterns of behavior aren't just descriptions of people you've never met before.

Chances are, you've seen one or more of these destructive behavior patterns—and you've lived to tell the tale. Fair warning: you might see parts of yourself inside these leadership attitudes. Because, as we will discover, these six archetypes—The Destructive Six—are parts of all of us. The good news is that where we are headed, the whole is always greater than the sum of its parts.

CHAPTER 3

MEET THE DESTRUCTIVE SIX

"Becoming a leader is synonymous with becoming yourself. It is precisely that simple and it is also that difficult."

— WARREN BENNIS, FORMER USC LEADERSHIP PROFESSOR AND AUTHOR OF LEADERSHIP JAZZ

"The depth of the darkness to which you can descend and still live is an exact measure of the height to which you can aspire to reach."

— PLINY THE ELDER, GREEK PHILOSOPHER

Have you ever experienced toxic leadership?

Let me ask you the same question in another way: Have you ever worked for a toxic boss? Okay—have you ever *been* that toxic boss?

I'm wondering if you've experienced a part of yourself that maybe isn't something you are necessarily proud of, but… There it is.

I know I've been the victim of more than one bad boss. Stabbed in the back, confused, wondering what I could have done differently. I've tasted the poison of toxic leadership. I've made it my life's work to help my clients overcome the damage of bad bosses, both externally and internally (inside of themselves).

From the school of hard knocks, where all the faculty are horrible, I came to a realization: what if my boss's behavior is not about me?

What if poor leadership is something that we see... everywhere? Even in parts of ourselves? Even within our own minds? External or internal, there are a lot of examples of poor leadership.

Perhaps you have worked for a horrible boss—or maybe you have a few in your head? There's no shame or blame in that remark. Just a simple observation: we are all fallible human beings. Nobody's perfect, not even a perfect fool. Sometimes bosses exhibit toxic traits—and sometimes, we aren't exactly kind to ourselves in our own minds.

In a world where nothing is static, everything is in constant motion, and uncertainty is all around us. From that uncertainty, we recognize chaos. But where, in a professional setting, does chaos come from? And where can we find a way to bring order to the chaos?

What's most soul-sucking for you?

What's most soul-sucking for you?

The author can see how you vote. **Learn more**

A*shole boss ✓	**67%**
A b*tch of a commute ✓	**11%**
Sh*tty growth prospects ✓	**9%**

IMAGE 2. 1. LinkedIn Poll Results

The real question is: how can we identify the behaviors of a destructive leader? These characteristics may be discovered through your own experience or the experience of others.

But in my experience, I prefer to turn to science. We must define what is destroying organizations and ruining careers. We scientifically diagnose the gaps so that we can transform the way we deal with our parts and expand our Self-leadership. We must create a new generation of leaders, so that self-directed work teams and other organizational structures can thrive in the age of AI.

There are six types of destructive leadership, according to a study conducted in Sweden, under the title of *Appetite for Destruction*. Research shows that the Destructive Six can rob leaders (and their teams) of productivity, efficiency, and progress—even eroding mental and physical health. Inside an organization, the Destructive Six are driving turnover, creating defensiveness, fostering mistrust, and robbing you of your impact. Notice that these six types of toxic leaders are not just archetypes—they are parts of us all. During times of chaos, the Destructive Six represent the parts of us that can take over—and take down an organization in the process.

Does anyone quit their job by saying, "My boss is so nice to me, every day! The clarity of direction and support here fills me with a sense of purpose. The kindness is overwhelming. Peace out and namaste, nerds—I quit."

No. Clarity, support, and purpose are why people stay. Not the reasons why people leave.

Science tells us that 65% of the working population has been exposed to destructive leadership. Beyond your personal experience, consider the characteristics and behaviors that are stealing profits from your organization, robbing you of efficiency, destroying collaboration, productivity, and more.

The Destructive Six are six parts within us—they manifest as patterns of behavior, designed to protect us from perceived fears or to drive us toward different results. Remember, like the capacity for joy, gratitude, and regret, we all possess these characteristics.

The key to being an effective leader is often found in restraint, redirection, and a new way of looking at the same old problems.

Fortunately, we don't have to show up the same way every day, without self-awareness. "That's just the way I am" is one of the biggest lies in business. We all have the capacity to be better. We all have the capacity to change. Neuroplasticity (the ability for our brains to rewire and find new approaches) exists. Otherwise, therapy wouldn't work. Coaching wouldn't work. And progress would never arrive.

"A strong, secure leader accepts blame and gives credit," according to the famous UCLA basketball coach, John Wooden. He goes on to say, "A weak, insecure leader gives blame and takes credit." Notice how that observation plays out, inside each of the Destructive Six. Because awareness is the first step towards change. When it comes to the Destructive Six, the intention is to protect. But in response to fear, insecurity, and other limited thinking, the result is chaos. Notice that matters get worse when we rely on our parts to protect the whole.

Bringing your whole self to work is where we need to land. But before we get further into Self-leadership, consider what its absence looks like.

The first type of toxic boss that comes to mind is the worst: Arrogant and Violent. Have you ever experienced a leader who turns to shaming, verbal abuse, screaming, and even physical confrontation? Have you been there?

Think of Gordon Ramsay with a toothache, and the soufflé doesn't have enough "souff." Fortunately, this pattern of behavior shows up less than 6% of the time. Rarely do leaders resort to "violence," but screaming, throwing things (including insults) gets you a seat in this most unwanted category.

"Workplace violence has received increased attention in the last decade, according to the National Library of Medicine in the United States. The International Labour Organization uses a definition of workplace violence adapted from the European Commission: "Incidents where staff are abused, threatened or assaulted in circumstances related to their work, including commuting to and from work, involving an explicit or implicit challenge to their safety, well-being or health."

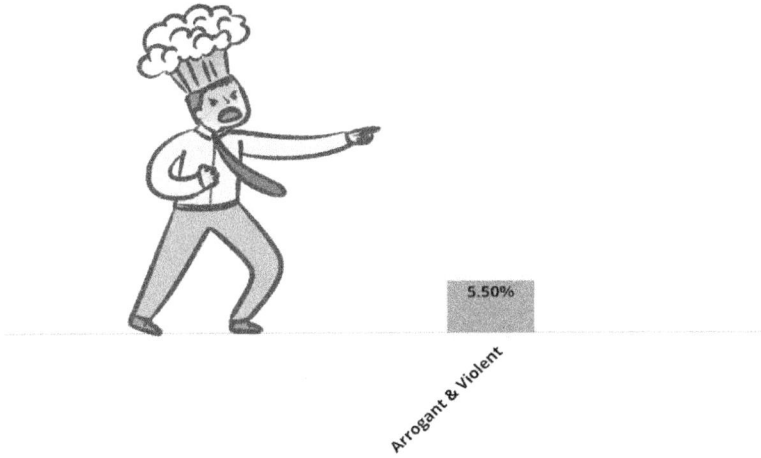

IMAGE 2.2. Arrogant and Violent—The Destructive Six

Notice how the arrogant and violent part is over-indexing. The severe over-correction on some perceived threat (which is really the "fight" response, when fear is triggered) goes too far—and the results can be disastrous.

When people are facing their fears, real or imagined, and chaos rules the day, violence can often be the result. In healthcare, for example, people are confronting real and life-threatening illnesses, injuries, and the loss of loved ones. In the practice of medicine, science confronts the unexpected—often the results (despite best efforts) are unpredictable. Inside this arena of service, healthcare workers are five times more likely to experience workplace violence than employees in any other industry. A survey from the American College of Emergency Physicians says that 91% of emergency room doctors have been the victims of violence in recent years. For nurses, according to a 2024 survey from National Nurses United, nearly 82% of nurses have experienced at least one type of workplace violence incident.

The American Psychological Association reports that teachers and school administrators are also experiencing greater violence in U.S. schools, especially after the pandemic. 80% of teachers report at least one incident of verbal harassment and threatening behavior from students. Only 1% of respondents reported violent encounters with parents before the pandemic, and less than 1% during the pandemic. After the pandemic, the number of violent incidents with parents jumped to 26%.

If you or someone you know is experiencing violence at home or in the workplace, don't wait to get help. Reach out to somebody and move towards personal safety. If you are in a dangerous space, recognize that it's okay to get away. When others are behaving badly, it's easy to think it's your fault and that you are the one who needs to change. It's not. Don't give in to gaslighting and blamestorming. You don't have to excuse bad behavior when your safety is threatened.

Change your circumstances, and don't be afraid to seek out coaching, counseling, therapy or even legal action—so that you can have a safe place where you can reflect and grow (without threats hanging over your head).

Just beside violent behavior, we find the next category. Almost 20% of employees have had a boss who uses threats and punishment to "keep people in line." That's the abusive narcissist.

These abusive narcissists are driven by ego and fear. As a result, they break their promises, generate mistrust, and think nothing of putting their name on your latest report. Andrew Carnegie, the great American industrialist and philanthropist, said, "No one will make a great leader who wants to do it all by him or herself—or get all the credit for doing it."

Cruelty is not communication. And scolding is not a strategy.

Some bosses take the opposite approach from aggressive and narcissistic behavior. Some parts make us reductive and cowardly. If these bosses were dogs, do you know what kind of dog they would be?

They would be cats.

And do you know where you could find these cats?

No one does. Because these cats are hiding. Hiding from what needs to be done, shirking their own authority, avoiding necessary input—and robbing you and your team of much-needed direction. These are the scaredy-cats, and you can spot them by their trademark phrases. "I don't want to get involved. It's upper management," they say. "Why don't you figure it out?" is another one, a phrase that's disguised as an effort to avoid micromanagement. But instead, putting the burden back on the employee, they avoid collaboration and input. Why?

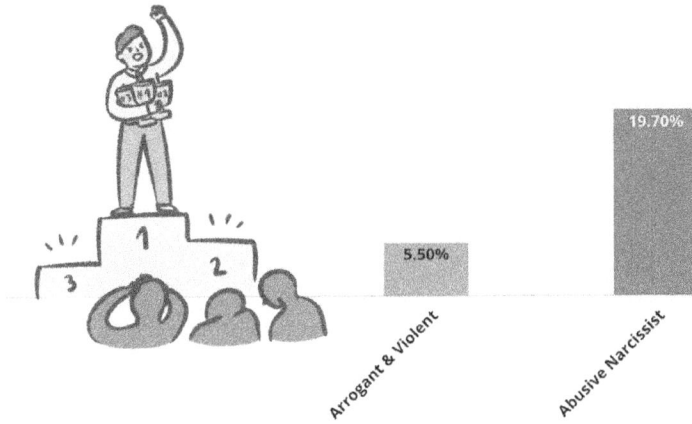

IMAGE 2.3. Abusive Narcissist—The Destructive Six

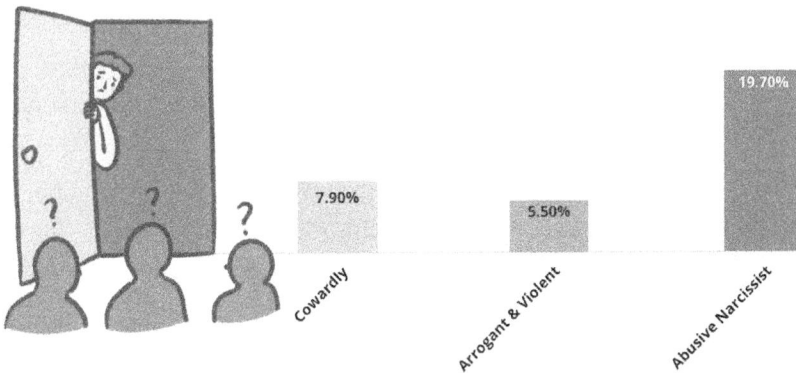

IMAGE 2.3. Cowardly Narcissist—The Destructive Six

My dog Sasha hiding under the couch from loud noises.

Unable to face even the simplest confrontation, accountability, or responsibility, these cats shy away from the conversations that matter, acting too passively and leaving a trail of mystery, confusion, and missed opportunities. (Maybe that's why I'm more of a dog person—but I still love my cat, Mowgli).

The cowardly internal part of ourselves says things like "I'm not qualified" or "this person is smarter than me." So, they back away, in a "flight" response to what is perceived as an overwhelming situation. Or, if someone is afraid of making a mistake, they can freeze as well. A version of a perfectionist part ("What happens if I get it wrong? Then I'll be in trouble!") can take over.

The cowardly leader is probably a good place to talk about fear. Notice the role that fear plays in these scenarios. When anyone is afraid, even on a small or minor level, the amygdala part of the brain kicks in. The result? Well, the amygdala controls the release of hormones, like adrenaline and cortisol—two stress hormones.

'When fear activates, the amygdala, a part of the brain's limbic system, triggers a cascade of responses to prepare the body for a perceived threat," according to Northwestern Medical Clinical Psychologist, Zachary Sikora, PsyD. "This [activation] can involve the release of stress hormones and the redirection of resources to the areas of the brain involved in survival, like the amygdala. As a result, other areas of the brain, particularly the prefrontal cortex (responsible for planning, decision-making, and rational thought), can be less active. This 'cognitive overload' can make it difficult to think clearly, make reasoned decisions, or even communicate effectively." If you've been alive for more than five minutes, I'm guessing you know exactly what this experience is like.

Beyond the release of chemical stimuli in response to strong emotions (fear), our human operating system also allows parts to take over. The combination of chemistry and parts can cause a variety of familiar responses—in fact, the Destructive Six arise as part of a fear response, on some level. And we see parts consume the whole, robbing the individual (and the organization) of leadership. Because, when parts take over, Self-leadership, and self-restraint, is in short supply.

Inside a fear response, parts show up around four types of behavior:

1. **Fight:** Getting aggressive or abusive
2. **Flight:** Turning away (or running away) from perceived risks and dangers
3. **Freeze:** Notice that the "deer in the headlights" often gets run over
4. **Fawn:** Another deer reference? Actually, this response means excessive flattery, insincere praise, or behavior designed for approval. I think of it as just people pleasing—like when your dog rolls over onto its back, as a sign of submission.

But I digress.

The fourth type in the Destructive Six is the Messy Leader. These folks are insecure in their role—think "imposter syndrome"—and suffer from an inability to structure and plan. Often, these are people-pleasers who can't be sure what their superiors want, so they try to give them everything.

Think of the villagers in *King Kong*, offering up a woman to the great ape as a human sacrifice, in hopes that it will curry favor and the massive monkey won't go berserk. But guess what? Watch any Kong movie of your choice and get ready for the scene where the big monkey loses it. No matter the sacrifice or the attempts to pacify the great ape, Kong *always* goes berserk. People pleasing, not unlike gorilla-pleasing, is absolutely bananas. You wanna know why?

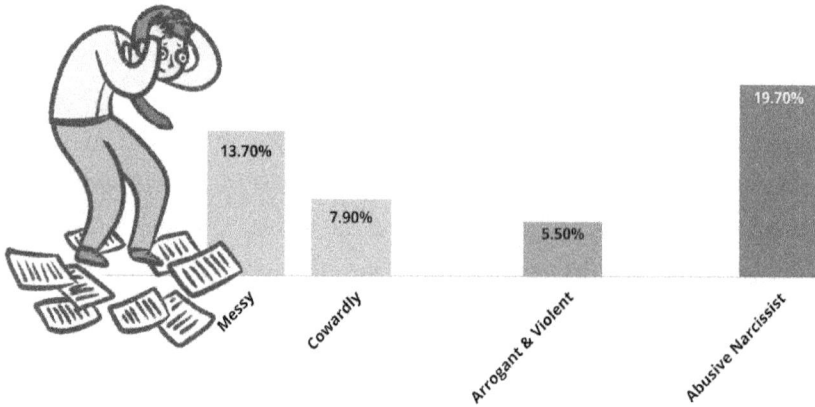

IMAGE 2.5. The Messy Leader—The Destructive Six

Because you can't please all of the people all of the time. "Fawning" is another word for this kind of behavior—trying to please people and gain favor, because of fear. The people pleaser makes a mess because they are unwilling to tell upper management (or team members) the truth. Boundaries aren't provided, guardrails shift, and the goal posts move yet again. To please the big boss, you (or your work) might have to be sacrificed.

Imagine an alarm clock that is afraid to really say what time it is. How's that gonna work? Terrified to disappoint someone, like an alarm clock that won't tell the truth, this kind of bad boss ends up disappointing everyone.

Under the messy leader, the team experiences lots of flip-flopping, indecisiveness, fire-fighting, and yes, even human sacrifice. Nearly 14%

of destructive leaders fit into this category, unable or unwilling to set boundaries and perpetually trying to please the biggest monkeys in the room. Fawning creates chaos on multiple levels.

The fifth and sixth types are combination types. Roughly 8% of destructive leaders fall into the category of passive-aggressive leadership, with 10% earning the title of "passive egocentric." Together, almost 20% of leaders are a combination of passive & active destructive behaviors.

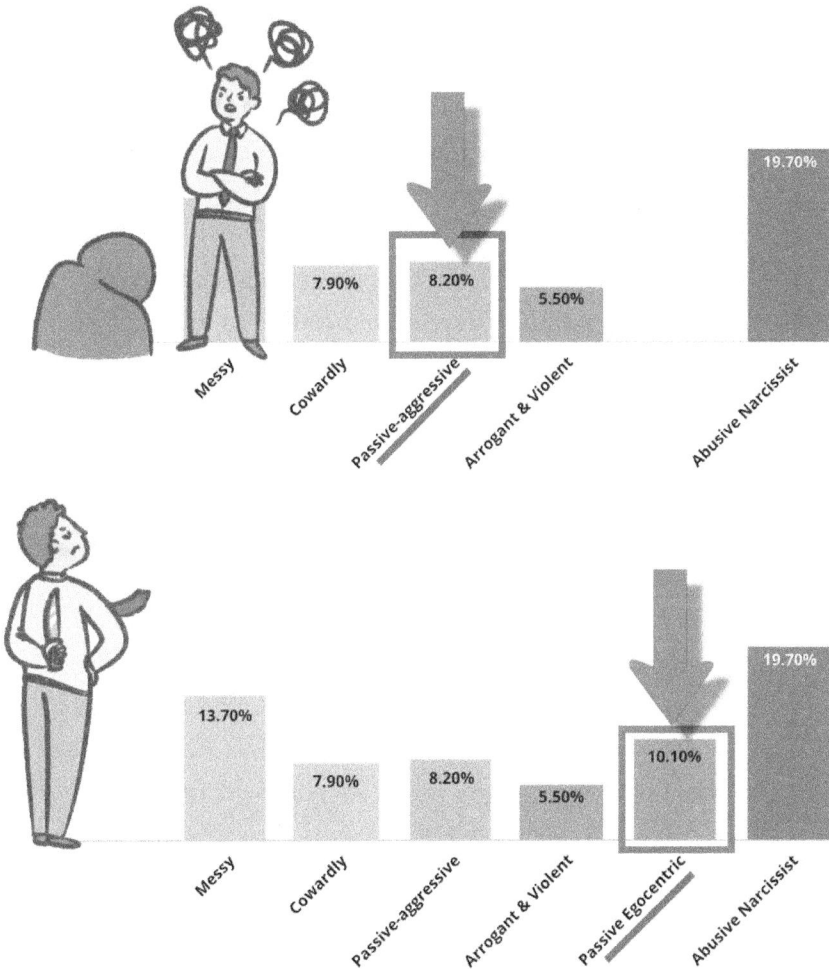

IMAGE 2.6. The Two Types of Passively & Actively Destructive Leaders—
The Destructive Six

How do you know if you are working with or have one of these passive & active combo parts? Look for subtle sabotage, deafening silence and/or a lack of clarity. *Psychology Today* says that there are four tell-tale signs:

1. **They speak in codes**: Often using sarcasm and verbal indirectness to convey a point. What point, you might ask? Well, that's for you to figure out, now isn't it? A degrading smirk, accompanied by silence, is the mode of operations here. These parts require you to play a guessing game around your performance, using facial expressions to convey their wishes while they doodle during meetings and check emails during zoom calls. Is side-eye an effective leadership strategy?

2. **Hyper-conforming:** Often used by parts to avoid taking action, it centers on the seven most dangerous words in business: "That's the way we've always done things." The hyper-conformist part says to toe the line—by getting back in line! Don't make waves, the hyper-conformist preaches. But what if those waves lead to... progress? Notice how these passive types abdicate responsibility: "I don't make the rules," they say, or "Listen, if it were up to me..." What's the effect of these empty phrases on employees? In my experience, platitudes don't help attitudes.

3. **Passing the buck:** Do you have a part that's in denial about the need for change, and unwilling to accept responsibility? Are you seeing small administrative changes that turn into massive challenges, where others are often "thrown under the bus" so that your part can keep things the way they are? What's the cost of passing the buck here? Progress, people, profits... the list goes on.

4. **Scapegoating:** Remember what John Wooden said about accepting blame? There's a reason the winningest basketball coach in UCLA history advocates for taking responsibility,

not accusing others, and offloading accountability. Do you have a part that's looking for a fall guy? Look, Ryan Gosling is great and that movie was a lot of fun, but when it comes to the workplace, nobody wants to be *The Fall Guy*. The passive-aggressive part is always on the lookout for a scapegoat, blamestorming instead of brainstorming for a new solution. At Nokia, one of my clients, one of their core values is creating a "no-blame" culture. What would that mean for your team and your organization? Have you experienced a lot of scapegoating at work?

Chances are, you have. The end result is pretty shocking: only about a third of workers are lucky enough to experience a leader who scores low on destructive leadership behaviors.

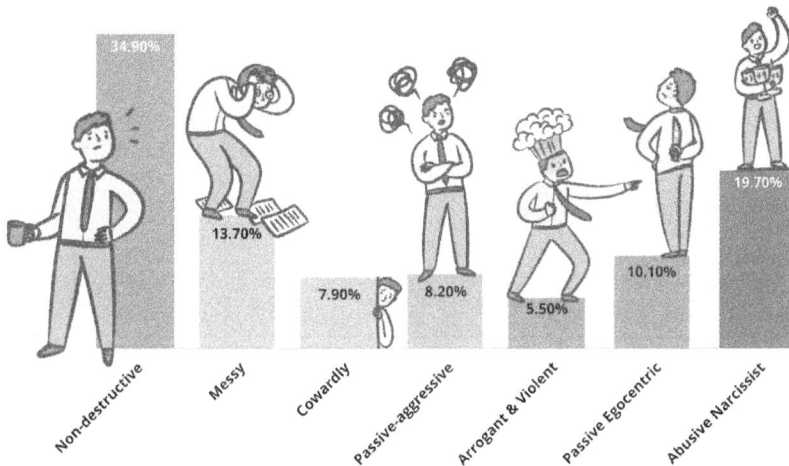

IMAGE 2.7. Almost 2/3 of Workers Experience Destructive Leadership Parts

But why would an organization—why would a leader—change? After all, there are those who say, "Why change the methods, if they get results?"

Here with a rebuttal is: Science. The data says that being toxic *doesn't* work. Especially when people stop working for you. Consider the Global Destructive Factor:

Global Destructive Factor
(lower is better)

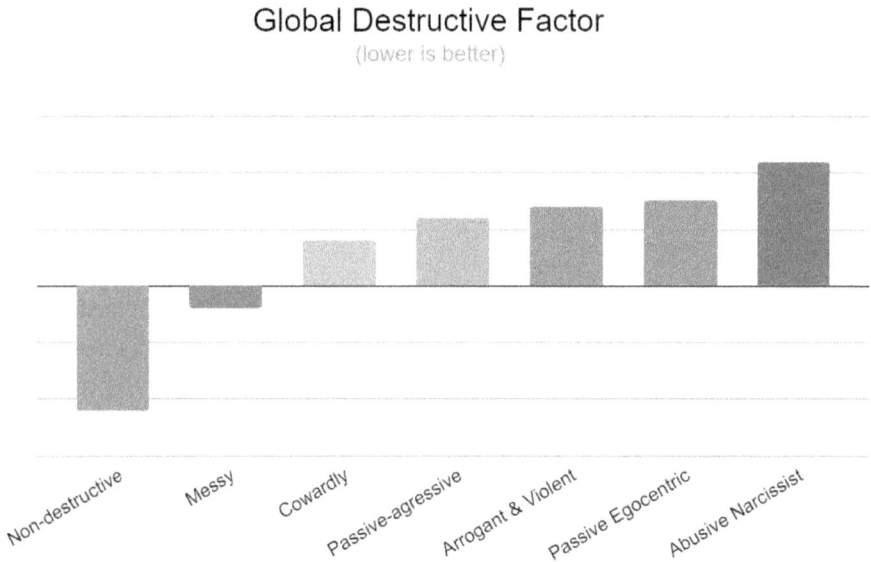

IMAGE 2.8. Global Destructive Factor—The Destructive Six

In this chart, from left to right, leaders do more good than harm. The further you move to the right, the more destructive the leader becomes. Leaders with low amounts of destructive behavior create long-term growth (not just short-term results). And as you can see from the chart below, even leaders with messy or conflict-averse parts can actually turn out okay. But overall, the more destructive the behavior, the more it lowers work performance, making job satisfaction plummet while employee burnout and turnover increase.

Boss profiles' long-term effect on workforce
(higher is better)

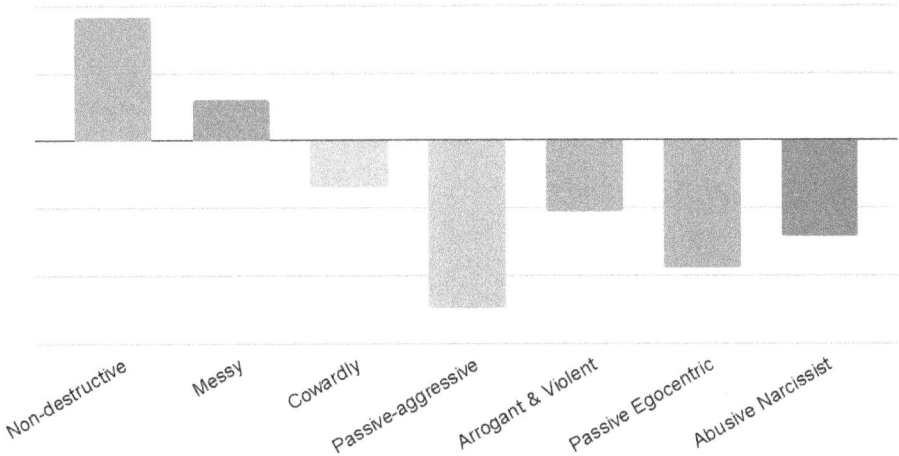

Non-destructive Messy Cowardly Passive-aggressive Arrogant & Violent Passive Egocentric Abusive Narcissist

IMAGE 2.9. Long Term Effects on Workforce—The Destructive Six

The University of Australia published a study that shows that *Toxic Workplaces Increase Risk of Depression by 300%*. And where you have greater levels of depression, you have higher rates of suicide. Toxic leadership is literally killing us.

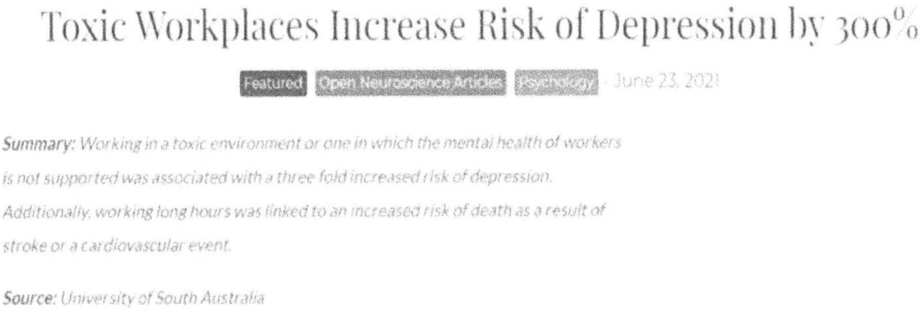

Toxic Workplaces Increase Risk of Depression by 300%

Featured Open Neuroscience Articles Psychology   June 23, 2021

Summary: Working in a toxic environment or one in which the mental health of workers is not supported was associated with a three fold increased risk of depression. Additionally, working long hours was linked to an increased risk of death as a result of stroke or a cardiovascular event.

Source: University of South Australia

IMAGE 2.10. University of Australia Study—The Destructive Six

The Sloan School of Business at my alma mater, MIT, published a study of 34 million online employee profiles—looking at the reasons why people leave an organization. The top reason wasn't salary—it was toxic corporate culture.

"Your supervisor is more important to your health than your family doctor," according to Bob Chapman, CEO of manufacturer, Barry-Wehmiller, paraphrasing a study from the Mayo Clinic. Indeed, Jeffrey Pfeffer (a Stanford professor who has studied the relationship between workplace stress and health) published a definitive paper on the subject of how toxic workplaces are destroying us. His work estimates that there were an extra 120,000 deaths in the United States due to harmful management practices. On top of this startling statistic, he estimates that the cost of workplace stress (the after-effect of abusive leadership) is approximately $190 billion per year—making the workplace the fifth leading cause of death, worse than Alzheimer's or kidney disease, according to the BBC.

Notice that you can't out-pay toxicity. Salary doesn't change personality. How much is enough when you are working for an impossible boss (even one in your own mind)? Would more money stop some kind of emotional freight train inside of you? Maybe more money will help someone to stay put. But for how long? How long can an individual take the poison—at the hands of a bad boss, or inside their own head? What kind of performance and engagement can you really expect when parts take over and fear is leading your organization? Maybe we are supposed to just grit our teeth as we obey the words of author Jocko Willink: "embrace the suck." Or is there a better way? Is there a way to overcome the Destructive Six?

When I started off in the working world, I thought I had it all. I had done everything right. I played on the Canadian Junior National Water Polo Team; I was a three-time NCAA Academic All-American and then graduated with a degree in Mechanical Engineering. My time in Boston—at MIT—is one that I will always treasure.

I got an engineering job in mining, and since I had a different background than the other engineers, I could identify opportunities that led me to save my company millions. I thought I was on the fast track to success. I thought I was on the fast track to happiness.

Then everything came crashing down.

On my quest for success, I lost myself. I was sabotaged by a terrible boss.

Just in case you were wondering how terrible—the experience nearly killed me. Literally.

My manager was a passive-aggressive leader. He was unclear, uncertain, and he avoided confrontation—a deadly combination, mixing three types of the Destructive Six. At the same time, nothing I delivered was ever good enough for him. "We've always done it this way" and "don't rock the boat" were his mottos. Sound familiar?

Unaware of the risks associated with a slow-acting poison, I took a dangerous dose of destructive leadership on a daily basis.

By chipping away at employees' confidence, passive-aggressive leaders are responsible for the highest rates of burnout and the lowest rates of job satisfaction. Research explains it but let me tell you: I have lived it. These passive-aggressive leaders make some people quit, while others turn in on themselves. After all, that's how poison works: it eats away at you from the inside.

I wasn't aware of it at the time, but I'd spent my entire life craving recognition and validation from my superiors. That recognition was what motivated me—the survival strategy I adopted without knowing it was driven by a part of me—the part that wanted to succeed. And it worked! Performing for coaches and teachers kept me striving, driving, and achieving. Staying in the pool at water polo practice when others were whimpering and calling it quits… It made me better—not worse. In the workplace, my approach was the same: I was driven.

Today, as I reflect on the past, I wonder: Was the pursuit of recognition a good thing or a bad thing?

Well, like most things, it was a question of external degrees. And internal awareness. When we meet the moment, as it is, we are effective. When our parts over-index, we suffer—and so do those around us. Here's what it looked like for me:

The mask I wore for the outside world was The Hard-Working Guy Who Delivers. "Reliable Rob."

In reality, I had no idea who I was. But I wore that mask for so long, I convinced myself that this character—this part—was my entire identity. Can you relate? I was existing as a persona, not a person. I was chasing a construct—a vision of success that my parts had created inside my own mind. The mask of Reliable Rob was all I knew. Instead of being something simpler and more real (myself), I was working so hard, like a robot, to hold up that masked persona. Behind the mask, all was chaos. Like a robot, I had no idea who I really was.

I was miserable—clinically depressed, to be precise.

Did I give too much of myself to an asshole boss, losing myself inside a toxic culture? Was my loyalty—my devotion to achievement—the real source of me spinning out of control? Why was happiness so scarce, and the achievement that had followed me throughout my athletic career so elusive at work? Enter the Destructive Six, inside my own head:

I had an abusive narcissist part that had helped me succeed in water polo and at MIT. I wasn't afraid to kick my own ass. That's how you get better at sports—you push yourself. But consider what happens when this part of me—the part that is driven to achieve and accomplish—isn't rewarded. It isn't even recognized. Effort and success were somehow separated, and inside of me: my parts were confused. One plus one didn't equal two; it equaled zero. I saw myself as the negative in the equation.

Trying harder was always my way—but when results didn't follow, chaos ruled my world. Nothing made sense! I wasn't "succeeding" at work (that was how my parts saw the situation). I became buried in negativity—frozen and uncertain, inside the chaos! Eventually, the lack of acknowledgement activated the arrogant and violent parts inside of me, which quickly led to self-destruction. Like a robot given a sheet of paper, and on both sides it says, "What is written on the other side is false." I was locked inside the liar's paradox—experiencing a gigantic loop that was causing my parts to turn inward in a very harmful way. If I can't solve this puzzle of achievement, my robot brain reasoned, I don't deserve to walk this earth!

(I'm not saying our parts are right. Or smart. Or useful. I'm just telling you my experience—and it was scary.)

What I came to realize, with therapy and self-reflection, was that it wasn't my circumstances that created the chaos inside of me. My situation didn't make me turn into someone I didn't recognize. I was making a contribution at work—it was *my boss* who didn't recognize it.

Notice that the chaos arrived as I internalized his lack of communication as a sign of personal failure. Nothing could be further from the truth, but my abusive part asked me to believe a lie—and then asked me to work harder to correct something that doesn't even exist! Does that sound like chaos to you? Chasing a phantom while taking your identity from non-existent feedback, so that your robot brain just chugs away at the idea that you aren't good enough? That was the chaos inside my world: damned if you do and damned if you don't, I kept looking for external inputs to create internal calm. And chaos was the result.

In order to create real change inside myself, and heal, I had to make a change. A change that would make me impervious to horrible bosses.

From this initial awareness, a journey of transformation began. I started to accept my parts—even the parts that were leading me down a very destructive path. Do you know why? Because my parts—like the parts inside of you—were only trying to help. But over-indexing on assistance, protection and analysis was a very dangerous place for me. Especially because of the way I had been treated by a toxic leader.

By triggering the parts that feel like I could never be good enough, my manager ground me down. Day by day, I questioned my choices at work, then my purpose, then whether my life itself had any meaning. I found myself on the edge of an abyss.

> *"He who fights with monsters might take care lest he thereby become a monster. And if you gaze for long into an abyss, the abyss gazes also into you."*
>
> —NIETZSCHE

I turned my gaze inward—into my own personal abyss. And I felt fractured. Broken. Unable to achieve because my boss kept moving the goalposts. Or hiding them altogether—inside of Nietzsche's abyss, perhaps? I kept looking into it.

It's easy to say, "Why not just quit?" But that's a naïve and simplistic answer to a complex problem. Reliable Rob wasn't a quitter. So I stayed at my post. I kept grinding. Working harder than ever. Cranking through chaos, not capitalizing on it.

Grinding is a sign of internal chaos. I always described it to my therapists as "I'm at war today." The abusive/violent parts were punishing me to the point of self-destruction. But something, something deep down, wanted to keep me alive. Somehow, there had to be a way for me to get better.

Ultimately, this internal chaos kept me small. Every day I was trying to survive, I wasn't creating, I wasn't growing, I wasn't expanding or evolving. I was a horse wearing blinders taking 1 step forward every day. Doing what I needed to do to get through as best as I could. "Reliable Rob," indeed.

"As best as I could" is the second piece. When you're trying to survive and your brain is in fear, you cannot access problem solving, new perspectives, innovation, expanded thoughts.

What does your organization want, and what do you deserve? The ability to think and reason and innovate and create—none of which is possible when you are trapped inside the fear and frustration of internal chaos.

The process in this book will help you to get better results, because of a deeper understanding that you are more than just your parts. You will be able to be creative, expansive, innovative, disruptive, and confident, regardless of your circumstances. That way, you can truly capitalize on chaos. That promise is not woo-woo, it's neuroscience.

As the saying goes, everywhere you go, there you are. There are always transition costs in any career—and no guarantees that you won't discover more chaos for you at your next go-round.

I viewed myself as a competitor, and I had the trophies and medals to prove it. Leaving my job would mean that my boss had won. And that "other" job with a fat salary is never just one click away, despite what LinkedIn might want you to believe.

My life—my work life—was killing me, and I didn't know how to change. It wasn't until I discovered how to work on myself that I was able to see through the chaos. To find the way back to myself, back to clarity, back to the place where I wasn't looking for my identity inside my circumstances. The transformation began inside a framework for realigning my goals with that elusive part of me: myself.

It's time to go beyond the Destructive Six and explore a framework that can help you move past whatever chaos you are facing right now. Beyond the misunderstandings of useless or non-existent feedback, you have the ability to navigate life in a new way. After all, you've made it this far—don't forget that. A new level of discovery can create calm inside even the most stressful circumstances.

You can regain your footing, even inside a toxic environment, and discover that chaos doesn't have to define you or destroy your ability to function, perform, and execute. The key to capitalizing on chaos comes from understanding—an understanding of what chaos really is.

And then: an understanding of the Self, with a capital "S," so that masks and obligations no longer obscure your identity.

Chaos is a label that we attach to a level of uncertainty. It's a word we use to categorize the apparent insanity of the world (and maybe the people) around us. There are many synonyms for chaos, but the best one I've found is probably confusion.

When we can't make sense of things—such as the behavior of a bad boss or the implementation of policies that don't seem to make sense—confusion can be the result. We look for certainty, but instead we find the unexpected. Despite our best plans, life is often unplanned. Is that chaos—or opportunity?

It depends on how you look at it. And how you respond to it.

Consider my current coaching client who wanted to triple his revenues in the next year—leaping from seven figures to eight, in short order. At first, the goal seemed like a pipe dream. Then, a customer opportunity came along that would allow just that—bringing somewhere in the range of $9-12 million USD to his company.

You could say that this unexpected opportunity was born out of chaos, as it was completely and totally unexpected. Nobody had that number on their sales forecast, balance sheet, or bingo card.

In order to capture that business, his organization would have to shift and transform into something completely unknown. Through our work, he discovered the need for project management expertise and hiring a few skilled people as the path to fulfillment—bringing order to chaos. Did he make that discovery because I pointed out the shortcomings in his supply chain? Was it because I shared with him a sixteen-step PowerPoint on the advantages of the PMP (Project Management Program) certification?

No. None of the above.

What helped him to 5X his revenues inside of 18 months is an opportunity that allowed for a deeper understanding, inside of a good kind of chaos. (Notice that chaos brings the unexpected, and sometimes that unplanned change is a welcome one!)

Notice how we navigated through the unknown and addressed the confusion. We didn't jump into tactics and strategies—we looked for understanding inside the situation. And that understanding began inside my client.

We began by looking at how we, as human beings, are wired. Before we jumped to engineering a solution, we addressed physics first. In other words, we looked at how things work (even in the midst of rapid and unpredictable change).

Instead of diving headfirst into the details around a business solution, we looked at the player inside the game. We found a way to introduce some tranquility into a hectic situation, so that he had the mental headroom to see things from a new viewpoint.

And new discovery occurred, as it does for all of us, when he got out of his own way. The chaos still remained—after all, life is always uncertain. No one can know everything, and nobody can predict the future. That's just physics: the way things work. But knowing how things work can help us make things work in our favor. Even amid chaos, complexity, and organizational transformation, the first step is always the first step.

From an understanding of the human operating system, you too can discover how to get out of your own way. Because when we identify our fears—those emotions that are designed to protect us but sometimes they end up imprisoning us—we find our way through the chaos. We find what's waiting on the other side of uncertainty.

Freedom.

A deeper understanding of the principles that have guided me—and hundreds of my clients—is the first step towards that freedom. The freedom to be who you are, beyond the chaos. The freedom to show up, as yourself, regardless of the chaos that surrounds you.

Why? Because this framework helps you—and your entire organization—capitalize on chaos.

BREAKDOWN TO BREAK THROUGH

In some chapters, I'll offer a summary of key themes, plus insights that can help you (and your organization) to implement new ideas. I call this summary, *Break Down to Break Through*. Here are some key ideas to recognize and remember:

1. Nearly two-thirds of the population has been exposed to destructive leadership. Bad bosses are in every organization right now. If you are experiencing toxic leadership, you are not alone.

2. If you are in a leadership role, you may be exhibiting behavior(s) of the Destructive Six (especially when you feel stressed, anxious, and/or afraid)! Remember, these personas are inside every person. You are responsible for yourself and your behavior, even in the midst of chaos. How are you stepping towards progress, away from the Destructive Six and towards success? (This book is a great start!)

3. Four of the Destructive Six are "actively destructive," meaning these poisonous people exhibit behavior that is detrimental, debilitating, and divisive. Two of the Destructive Six are not intentionally harmful, but they create mayhem and confusion (another word for "chaos") nonetheless. These two types are the Cowardly Part and the Messy Part. These two types are examples of leaders that can't get out of their own way—and as a result, they end up getting in your way. Unlike the other members of the Destructive Six, the intentions are different with these two types. But the result (restricted growth, personnel issues, confusion, poor communication and more) is the same.

The coming chapters will take a deeper look at each of the Destructive Six, offering insights and guidance on the antidote for these toxic behaviors—inside yourself and inside your organization.

EXPLORATIONS

1. Which of the Destructive Six have you experienced?
2. Which have you demonstrated? Can you identify any of these behaviors as your own?

3. If you had to select one or two of the Destructive Six parts that show up in you the most often, which ones would they be? Which ones best describe the team members around you, your board members and/or your investors?

4. If you are using this book to coach team members, it may be useful to share stories where chaos was created by a toxic leader. Chances are you don't have to go far to find a leader that thrives on chaos— or seems to create it wherever they go. If you are a coach, or leader acting in that capacity, ask your client (or team member—choose the words that fit for you) how they reacted and responded to the chaos that came from others.

5. For group coaching: if you are encouraging group discussion inside an organization, recognize that people may not be willing to share—because they might be surrounded by toxicity right there in the room! What can you do to facilitate a more open and directed conversation?

6. While internal coaching can be useful, it's tricky to be both leader and coach, if your "coaching clients" are your employees. Teams must create an environment where the conversation isn't nested in potential conflicts of interest between leadership and employees. After all, if a team member needs to talk to their coach about their boss, and their boss is their coach, how's that going to work? That's confusing—and counter-productive. How are you working to provide a safe space, where the conversation can go beyond chaos?

CHAPTER 4

RECONNECTION

> *"Seek out that particular mental attribute which makes you feel most deeply and vitally alive, along with which comes the inner voice which says, 'This is the real me,' and when you have found that attitude, follow it."*
>
> — WILLIAM JAMES, CONSIDERED ONE OF THE FOUNDERS OF MODERN PSYCHOLOGY

From time to time, we exhibit behavior that Robert Sutton called "temporary assholes." Sutton is the author of *The No Asshole Rule*. In his book, he goes on to identify persistently nasty and destructive jerks as "certified assholes"—thus distinguishing people we just don't like from those who have earned a higher designation for their consistently low behavior. But sometimes, the real asshole is inside our head: the part of us that's saying we aren't good enough, and creating a crisis of confidence!

We all know that we have the ability to be assholes—the part of us that is cruel, insensitive and destructive. We all can have the occasional bad day, or bad moment—when a part of us takes over and we treat others (or ourselves) badly. The question is: why can't we find a way to calm down these parts of ourselves? Why do we have to make more chaos when our parts take over? And, inside an organization, why can't these assholes just… change?

The effects of these certifiable assholes (surrounding us, or inside of us) are disastrous, not because of one enormous attack but because of hundreds—or even thousands—of small ones. The Destructive Six are creating chaos inside of companies—and individuals—all around the world.

A pattern of toxic behavior is "death by 10,000 cuts." As demeaning and dismissive parts (or people) rob us of our energy, our self-worth, and our motivation. It's well-documented that people in good moods are more productive, more creative, more receptive to feedback… the list goes on. But the inverse of the equation is also true. One destructive part (of a company or a person) can rob entire departments of their effectiveness. The most dangerous enemy is the one on the inside, right? Whether inside your organization or inside your own head, these parts need to be dealt with if we are going to find order inside chaos.

"These parts are not imaginary or symbolic," Dr. Schwartz says, addressing the facets inside our personality that can either help or harm. He thinks of these parts as individuals. "They are individuals who exist as an internal family within us," and he adds, "The key to health and happiness is to honor, understand, and love *every* part." [emphasis mine]

Indeed, in my research and work with clients, I have discovered that learning to love the various pieces and parts of our personalities can reintroduce new levels of understanding, healing, and prosperity. In fact, understanding how to identify and accept our psychological parts is the key to changing behavior and finding new ways to show up inside the same old circumstances.

IFS is a powerful paradigm because it gives all of us—assholes and non-assholes—a new approach to healing ourselves, our companies, and even our relationships.

"Our parts can sometimes be disruptive or harmful," Dr. Schwartz says, "but once they [our parts] are unburdened, they return to their essential goodness."

Winston is unburdened. Always.

He never leaves his essential goodness. Not even for a moment.

His round brown eyes are always open for new ideas, even if those ideas involve tearing down a tree with his teeth.

That's right, this bright labradoodle knows what you and I often forget: when we are true to ourselves, we are truly at our best. And Winston—my dog—is the best dog in the world.

To be fair, many of Winston's habits are things I do not recommend. The boy can't really feed himself, for example. Digging through garbage—with the accompanying mess that greets us when my wife and I come back home—is big fun for him. For us, not so much.

Do you know what IS big fun for me? Getting to learn from Winston, because he is a great reminder of what resilience and new possibilities look like.

Nothing gets him down! He's never preoccupied. Winston is not trying to come to terms with the past. He wants to play. He wants to get in the game, right now—whether that game is chasing a stick or barking at birds. Winston, the picture of emotional well-being, is always engaging with life *right now.*

Flow state? That's his natural state!

To be fair, his personality—his psychology—is a lot less complicated than yours or mine. His obligations and life requirements are a lot different than ours, too.

The simplicity of Winston's life is a beautiful thing. The good news is, you and I don't have to get down on all fours in order to experience our true selves. We simply need to understand our various parts, so that we can reclaim our *essential* wholeness.

Because when we return to our true selves, we discover Self-leadership—a kind of resourcefulness (dare I say "playfulness?") where we are resilient, resourceful, and connected. (I'll explain why that "S" is capitalized in a minute).

Winston

The other day, I took Winston out for a walk. He tore himself away from me, made a sudden beeline for the bushes, bit down, and started pulling with all his might. When I caught up with him, I finally saw what he was doing. My 30-pound labradoodle was trying to devour a 30-foot ash tree.

So I'm looking at my dog, chomping away at the tree. And I tried everything to make him stop. Asked. Begged. Yelled. Pulled his leash.

I finally gave up and sat down, feeling angry, powerless, and frustrated. I felt like a complete failure. How can I teach Fortune 500 companies management skills when I can't manage my frickin' dog?

And then it hit me. I was the problem.

What I realized that day was that the situation—of the terrible tree—had nothing to do with the dog. The problem was with the guy trying to "manage" him.

Instead of focusing on how things should be, I had to take the first step. I have to recognize Winston for what he is: a dog fighting with a tree. That's not a ridiculous situation unless I make it into one. I asked myself a powerful coaching question:

What else could this be?

It sparked another:

What happens if I accept Winston... as he is?

What happens if, instead of trying to manage him or turn him into something other than exactly who he is, I decide to meet him where he is—instead of where he should be?

I discovered I needed to give Winston what he always gives to me: acceptance. The first step to true and lasting change isn't screaming, or some other form of command and control bullshit. You have to accept what is, before you can change it.

We see that we have to accept nature, right? We look at a flock of birds, or the waves hitting the shore, and we see the perfection. The trees lose their leaves in the fall, and we reach for the rake. Nature is natural, right? We accept it.

Why can't we find the same acceptance inside our human nature? What would happen if we did? Without acceptance, there is no growth. No progress. And no fun! If you want to change a situation—or change yourself—it's best to begin by accepting where you are. Like a GPS that takes you where you want to go, you first have to identify your current location—your current situation—and accept it!

HUMAN NATURE = HUMANS IN NATURE

When we accept who we are, all of our parts that make up the whole, everything changes. We discover a new way of behaving within ourselves that connects our creativity to our own innovation, where we are stronger in the face of adversity. We no longer live from the limitations of the amygdala, where fight and flight rule the day. We can find space for creative problem solving. Professional insight. Innovation.

In other words, the kinds of things that your organization wants and your career deserves. Personal growth is the focus here, and it can't happen when we are frozen with fear, ruled by our parts, and unaccepting of ourselves. We are here to capitalize on chaos, not be overwhelmed by it. It's counterintuitive, but the journey to personal growth doesn't start with grit, fault-finding, or other kinds of aggressive introspection. The journey through chaos begins with compassion.

The key to dealing with chaos isn't brutal honesty—it's *compassionate* honesty.

Sometimes parts of us jump into action, and they can make assholes out of all of us. We over-index, overreact, over-protect… It's not a sign of your failure as a human. It's a sign that you *are* human! In my life, I've seen how my protector parts responded to fears that didn't exist, leaping towards imaginary problems and perceived threats. I know now that my parts turned my personal drive for success into a weapon, literally leading me to think of suicide! If you find times in your life where it seems that a part of you is trying to run your life, believe me, I've been there!

You are not alone. Replacing shame with compassion was my journey, and it helped me to heal. When I saw the parts of myself for what they were, I was able to accept these parts. And from acceptance, I came to trust myself—my true Self—because my parts were welcome as vital elements of my whole being.

Can you embrace the parts of yourself that only want the best for you, even though it may seem like the source of chaos in your life?

This exercise can help:

1. Reflect on a recent situation that caused you "negative" feelings (anxiety, fear, anger, sadness, frustration, etc.). I put "negative"

in quotations because these feelings aren't actually a bad thing. As Dr. Schwartz calls them, they are trailheads. And by exploring the trail, we learn & grow.

2. If it feels safe, lean into that feeling with curiosity and ask the feeling: What is it trying to tell you? How is it trying to help you? What is it protecting you from?

3. Give it love & compassion. The feeling—the part—may say hurtful or untrue things to you. You can imagine it as a child, so you can access compassion. That can help you to understand where the feeling is really coming from. In this dialogue, you can even ask the part how old it is, how it's trying to help you, and what its "job" is.

4. Ask it what you can do to make it feel safe. In many cases, it wants you to connect with it more often, so you can build trust. My clients tell me that this is like reconnecting with a person where the relationship drifted apart. That's been my experience as well.

For more guidance and an audio file that can walk you through this exercise, visit www.robkalwarowsky.com/chaos.

From this place of Self-leadership, we see new possibilities from a place of strength and compassion. From a unified perspective—where Schwartz's parts come into a unified whole—we see our circumstances differently. We don't have to revert to asshole behaviors or become victims of chaos (either internal or external). There is another way. Change is wired into everyone's psychology, even those of us who kick and scream when asked to confront it. Acceptance and compassion open the door to rebuilding, even in the midst of chaos.

In this journey back to ourselves, we find the joy that my teacher, Winston, experiences. When he is chasing a stick, lounging on my back porch, or jumping into a stream, Winston is always present and alive—teaching me what good looks like.

Why was Winston's behavior kicking my head in? Answer: It wasn't. Until I made up a story about how he "should" be behaving. I decided to leave the shoulds and shouldn'ts behind. When I learned to stop being an asshole, I started to enjoy my dog.

The way I love Winston is the way we need to love ourselves.

Does this sound strange to you? Maybe you've never learned from a labradoodle. I recommend you try it right away. It might help you to clear some trees, both literally and metaphorically.

While your life may not seem as easy and carefree as jumping into a stream, or lounging on the back porch, notice that "easy" and "carefree" are states of mind.

When you discover a new state of mind, what happens?

Your approach to the world, and the people in it, changes.

Sutton, in the *No Asshole Rule,* reminds us that, "psychologists make the distinction between states (fleeting feelings, thoughts, and actions) and traits (enduring personality characteristics) by looking for consistency across places and times—if someone consistently takes actions that leave a trail of victims in their wake, they deserve to be branded as certifiable assholes." For the rest of us, changing our state of mind is where true transformation begins. I would argue that changing a pattern of behavior begins with a shift in state of mind—and that shift can be as simple as a change in your point of view.

Have you ever been in the middle of a chaotic situation, and yet you felt calm? Ever been working super-hard but it doesn't feel like work at all? How about when a small request becomes "the last straw"—and suddenly the entire world looks like an error that needs to be corrected?

Sometimes people say things and we get triggered, while others just get on with their lives. How is that possible? How can these anomalies exist—different responses to similar situations?

The fact is: preference matters, and perspective matters. In my coaching practice, with CEOs, entrepreneurs, Olympic gold medalists and more, the greatest gift I can offer is my perspective. And when that perspective creates a new way of looking at things, clients change. Cultures change. A preference for progress emerges.

Does this evolution happen because I possess super-powers? Or because I'm magic? Hey, I'm from Canada, not Krypton. Change doesn't happen from magic. True and lasting change happens from a new level of internal understanding. Another way to say internal understanding? *Insight.* That's what I bring to my clients, via compassionate honesty—and what I want to bring to you.

From one to many, this understanding can change entire teams and even entire corporate cultures, helping everyone to capitalize on chaos. And that change happens from the inside out.

Turns out, the way we are on the inside is how we respond to the world on the outside. Let's consider an example—the difference between *overwork* and *overwhelm*:

Overwork can happen to anyone. That's when you are triple-booked and asked to do the work of two people before lunchtime. Like an electrical circuit flooded with a level of electricity that exceeds capacity, it's too much to handle. We can't be in two places at once, or create a fresh spreadsheet while simultaneously delivering a presentation. When circumstances are more than you can handle—you are overloaded.

But *overwhelm* is different. Overwhelm can happen when you can't find your car keys. Or pick out an outfit for the meeting tomorrow. Or respond to Trevor's text. Overload comes from circumstances. Where does overwhelm come from?

Notice that state of mind governs the way that we see the world. Is it chaos, or opportunity? Disaster, or minor inconvenience? Your point of view matters, and it can change with a thought. That's why it's so vital to see the world inside ourselves with a fresh perspective.

Otherwise, you'll leave Trevor on read, and is that what you really want?

No one does well under pressure or discouragement. That's what overwhelm feels like. Until the feeling goes away. When that part of you calms down, you can get moving again.

What would it mean to you if you could learn about and reduce your personal triggers and blind spots? How about accessing a clear vision for yourself and your life?

Human beings are multi-faceted, and the way we treat ourselves influences the way we treat others. According to Dr. Schwartz, inside each of us are three categories of parts—subpersonalities that can be experienced in thoughts, feelings, sensations and more. These parts develop complex systems of interaction among themselves, often carrying "burdens."

In general terms, these parts are developed to help us cope with circumstances and situations in the world around us. Schwartz breaks it down like this:

1. "Exiles" are parts of us that have experienced trauma and carry a burden of shame and/or pain. These are most often child parts that were hurt early in our lives.

2. "Managers" are the parts of our personality that run the show. These Managers attempt to keep control in situations and relationships, in an effort to keep the individual from feeling hurt or rejection. The manager parts work hard to pre-empt painful situations. If you struggle with being a perfectionist—in order to avoid embarrassment or blame—you might be experiencing a manager takeover. These parts are the drivers for behaviors like judgment (both external and internal), people-pleasing, high-achieving, controlling, pessimism, avoidance, and more.

3. "Firefighters" are a group of parts that react when Exiles are activated (triggered). Like a good firefighter, they try to extinguish the flames of emotion—sometimes turning to alcohol, drugs, or other harmful behaviors to keep the Exiles away. The Firefighters have 3 Ds of responses: distract, douse, and dissociate.

   a. Distraction can be anything from online shopping to Netflix binges.

    b. "Dousing the flames of emotion" can be behaviors from eating comfort food to addiction of any type. The most extreme version of dousing is suicide.

    c. Dissociation is when your mind disconnects from your feelings. This occurs when the suffering becomes very severe, and your mind separates you from emotion to protect you.

These parts are protective, which means that they are designed to help and serve you. According to *Forbes,* "The goal of IFS therapy is to help people identify and accept the different parts of themselves and heal the parts that are wounded. This can lead to personal growth and correcting problematic behavior patterns."

Notice that none of the parts are "bad." The goal of IFS isn't to remove any of the parts. The objective is balance—making sure that none of the parts are responding in an extreme way, taking over the actions and the conversation in a way that aids in asshole behavior.

Change can only occur in one place and in one place only, and that is inside ourselves. We can't change someone else's mind—but we can always change our own. Notice what Viktor Frankl wrote in *Man's Search for Meaning*: "When we are no longer able to change a situation, we are challenged to change ourselves." Want to shift out of chaos? Shift your perspective.

Change was possible, Frankl discovered, even inside a brutal and intolerable environment. (He spent time in four concentration camps—his wife and parents all died at the hands of the Nazis). Can you imagine that kind of horrific chaos?

Frankl couldn't take the guns from the guards, but he was able to find a way to persevere. Just as we all have the ability to be temporary assholes, we all have the ability to make choices—choices to change ourselves. To embrace who we are and find some compassion for all the facets of our personalities. To recognize what's really going on, so that our over-indexing parts can find trust instead of trauma.

And we can avoid creating more chaos.

More importantly, IFS seeks to bring us back to our Self. That's your true Self, right there—the place where you treat yourself with compassion and trust, and where the sum of your parts is greater than the whole.

While some might encourage you to "believe in yourself," I have a different question. Do you *trust* yourself?

From a place of acceptance, our parts—our internal families—learn to trust the Self. Our true Self. And when there is alignment and trust, bad behavior doesn't have to rule the day. Doubt and insecurity don't have to determine our behavior. When we understand why our Protectors are trying to protect us, there is no fire. We see that micromanaging is not good management.

From insight, we understand that there's another way. We trust ourselves to find our way back to Self. And we show up differently, as a result.

From an aligned identity, we find strength in the face of adversity. That strength allows us to avoid asshole behaviors—and remain resilient—because our parts can trust the Self.

CHAPTER 5

ARROGANT AND VIOLENT CHAOS

"Violence is the last refuge of the incompetent."

— ISAAC ASIMOV, AUTHOR OF FOUNDATION, AND I, ROBOT, AND
OVER 500 OTHER BOOKS

*"Winners are just people who have gone through
failure and have responded better than the rest."*

— AARON GORDON, PROFESSIONAL BASKETBALL PLAYER, DENVER NUGGETS

I often wonder why dogs bark. Have you ever asked yourself this question?

The simple answer is: because they are dogs.

But, as I reflect on this simple answer, I notice my canine teacher is looking at me. Winston, sitting in the corner, is not barking right now.

In fact, he's in his favorite sleeping pillow—we call it "The Launch Pad"—and he's looking up at me. He may be resting, but I never know when he might be ready to chase something. Or try to tear down a tree. While it's true that dogs bark, this dog is not barking at this moment.

Dogs, driven by instinct, will bark. Some more than others. While we can learn a lot from a labradoodle, the thing that strikes me is: you and I are not dogs. We are not driven purely by instinct. We have the capacity to keep calm when a package arrives at the front door. We don't need to lose our shit when guests come into the house.

Are you with me? The story continues:

Some dogs bite.

Thomas Gibson had it all. Born in South Carolina, he took an interest in the performing arts as a child. His talent and tenacity led him to earn a degree in theater from Juilliard, and he quickly became a mainstay in film and television work. He appeared as the title character (Greg) in the television series *Dharma and Greg* for nearly 120 episodes. Can you imagine what that experience was like? "Life on top of the world" is what comes to mind—a lead actor in a hit TV show! Wow.

In 2005 he was cast as Agent Aaron Hotchner, the lead in a new television series, *Criminal Minds*. His star continued to rise. He went on to appear on the series for an astonishing 11 years as the widely-loved lead investigator known to fans as "Hotch."

But in the 12th year... anger came on the scene. Actually, it had been there—playing in the background—for several years. Gibson's on-screen intensity had a dark side, chronicled in multiple incidents during his time on the show. His anger and outbursts were startling to people on set, according to multiple sources, but ignored by management because... well... what do you think?

Money.

Making a hit TV show is a huge money maker. And supporting the star is the secret of that success, right?

Maybe you don't work in Hollywood. Nevertheless, I bet you have seen how organizations can look the other way when there's bad behavior from a superstar. Especially violent behavior. Because somebody is an MVP, that means they can't be bridled, counseled, coached, or disciplined. Because their intensity drives success.

So, "You take the good with the bad"—until you can't take it anymore. In the case of *Criminal Minds*, bad behavior was seen as an unfortunate (but acceptable) by-product of a superstar operating at a high level.

That dark underbelly is just "par for the course" when dealing with a dynamic leader, dominant subject matter expert or, perhaps, the star of a hit television show. But beyond that unfortunate misunderstanding is a hard truth:

Functioning with intensity, in the pursuit of excellence, doesn't require violence.

And yet, for some, they can't seem to find another option.

Just before the holidays, Gibson was working on an episode of *Criminal Minds*. The crew was on location in downtown Los Angeles, on the Sixth Street Bridge. Gibson was driving a car across the bridge, and there was confusion about when he was supposed to take off in the car, according to *Variety*. After he crossed the bridge, he jumped out of the car, furious at the confusion. That was when he decided to showcase the worst parts of his emotional range.

Racing out of the car, he confronted and shouted at the director. Toe to toe, the director yelled back. Fed up, Gibson pushed the director with both hands.

According to *Variety*, Gibson had established a pattern of violent and unacceptable behavior. He received a DUI, pleading no contest to charges, in a prior year. Staff members described his behavior as "mercurial." Perhaps you've heard this word used to describe artists— or assholes—elsewhere?

Typically, when you see someone turning to violence there are other warning signs—other indicators and stressors that can influence behavior.

But I note that not everyone who experiences tough circumstances and workplace confusion has to resort to violence. Or, perhaps I should say, "micro-violence." Maybe nobody gets pushed, or punched, but microaggressions are still there. Demeaning and belittling comments, disrespect, and even threats can be a part of micro-violence in the workplace. Have you been there?

We all need to be aware of behavior that shows we are sliding into a dangerous place. Increasing your self-awareness is the first step—that means being willing to listen. Listening is leadership. Listening to coaches, spouses, colleagues, friends is how we turn feedback into a gift. Keep an open mind and see what's evolving—and listen to the resources you trust. Sometimes it's useful to take a look at the "moment before"—the moment before your parts take over.

Have you noticed any common themes when you explode? For me, it's when things don't go in the ways that "I expect" or when I've lost "control." Unfortunately, that's exactly what chaos is. We feel out of control, so we lose control.

I yell at the refs when I'm watching sports. I explode when I accidentally break a dish. Sometimes, I'm an asshole boss when Sasha (one of my dogs) runs off chasing a cat, cows or goats (yes, I live in a farming community). I don't chalk it up to "that's just me." My wife gave me feedback that she noticed an increase in this behavior and I'm working on it with my therapist as well as internally on my own time. Just as I am constantly improving, you can too.

After he was dismissed, Gibson said, "I love *Criminal Minds* and have put my heart and soul into it for the last twelve years. I had hoped to see it through to the end, but that won't be possible now. I would just like to say thank you to the writers, producers, actors, our amazing crew, and, most importantly, the best fans that a show could ever hope to have." While some on the show reported that they never saw the dark side of his personality, others said that people never knew which Thomas Gibson (or which part of Thomas Gibson) was going to show up.

Do I know Thomas Gibson? Do I know his challenges and issues? No, I do not. And let me be clear: I'm not saying that Thomas Gibson is anything other than a talented actor whose behavior cost him his job. There seems to be a protector part that took control, on more than one occasion, and his career felt the consequences.

While I don't know him, I know what violent behavior looks like. And according to witness accounts, and police reports, Gibson fell victim to a series of actions that led to his dismissal. There's always a part inside of any of us that has the potential for chaos.

Evidently he was going through a divorce at the time of the incident on the bridge.

So, I wonder: Are circumstances an excuse for literally pushing people around?

The answer is: No. Never.

There is another way.

Notice that what you have is not who you are.

You can have all the trappings of success. Wealth. Fame. A beautiful family.

And yet, our minds can get the best of us—if we allow it to happen. Then, what shows up is the worst of us. Our protector parts try to make things better, but they end up scorching the earth and burning the people who we care about—like the writers, staff, and directors who were a part of Gibson's success. That is, until he torched it all.

We all have our baggage. We all have our parts. And those protector parts can rush to our rescue, leading us to act without thinking. Instinct takes over. Especially when the pain of divorce, change or other loss can seem to threaten our identity.

Like a dog that turns a bark into a bite.

The good news is: you and I are not dogs.

When it comes to looking at the arrogant and violent origins of chaos, we have to remember one thing: human beings have the capacity to change. We don't have to show up the same way—especially if that way is self-absorbed and violent—inside our circumstances.

And, to be clear, if you are in a relationship or situation that is putting you in harm's way: find help. You don't have to put up with violence and abuse. There are a number of resources available, including human resources, at your company. Check the end of this chapter for additional ideas, or head to your web browser to tap into the latest resources.

You may be wondering if the executives at *Criminal Minds* wanted Gibson to change. According to reports, he was counseled. Sent to anger management classes. But exposure to classes is not the same as the choice to learn.

While we all have the capacity to change, the key to any transformation begins with choice. We must choose to be different—and that choice is within your grasp.

Especially if you find yourself working with an arrogant and violent co-worker, board member, or investor. There are steps that you can take to deal with this most sinister of the Destructive Six. While the arrogant and violent part makes up the smallest percentage, often this kind of behavior can do the most damage. One thing to remember:

You don't have to go it alone.

As you continue on your life's journey, let me share some of the things that I have come to understand about the violent aspects of the Destructive Six. Based on what I have applied, for myself and for my clients, I have come to a new understanding of not only where this behavior is coming from, but also a framework for addressing the real chaos here.

I notice that Winston is always going to bark at squirrels on our walks. But, as the one with the leash, I remember: I get to choose how I respond to those squirrels. And, for the record: Winston is a good dog who loves people. He might bark, but he does not bite. He's more of a lover than a fighter. But I digress.

Anger and even violence can come to us all, regardless of our circumstances. But remember: you are not your circumstances. Money, title, fame: none of it matters if we are out of touch with our true Selves. Without reconnection, our parts can rule the day—and create unwanted chaos.

Thomas Gibson was living in the stratosphere, in terms of professional accomplishment. He had achieved a level of success that few ever see or experience. But achievement is never enough if you don't see yourself as being enough.

While I am not a violent person, I can definitely relate to that dark place—that feeling of not being enough. A place where it seems there are no other options. Where life starts to look like a tiny, dimly lit room where the walls are closing in all around you. That feeling can cause your protector parts to rush forward, ruling your behavior and lashing out at what seems like insurmountable circumstances. I have the broken dishes to prove it.

But options—possibilities—always exist, right? Think about it: in this moment, as you read these words, how many possibilities exist? You can stop what you're doing. You can make a sandwich. You can call a friend, surf the web, or go walk the dog.

Whatever. My point is: possibilities always exist. And those possibilities are limitless. The challenge occurs when we forget that we have options. Maybe you can't go catch a flight to London right now, fly an airplane, or run General Motors—maybe that's not a possibility—but the number of possibilities that are available to you, regardless of your circumstances, are always and truly unlimited. I wonder, what are you forgetting right now—when it comes to your options and choices? Our parts don't want us to answer that question!

Our protector parts don't see possibilities. They see only danger. Fear. And their "best behavior" response, if unchecked, often brings out the worst in us.

I know what can happen when our parts rule the whole. We forget ourselves. And we can lose what is most important to us, if we turn to violence.

As I look back on my own personal journey, I recognize that I was never violent. I did not lash out at others. I didn't scream or rip into my fellow team members. I did not raise my fists or push someone.

Instead, I pushed myself. I let my dark passenger take the wheel, and I began driving myself into the depths of despair. While it's true I didn't lash out at others, it's also true that I lashed out… at myself.

Working for hours on end. Working out for even more hours on end. I pushed myself to the point of punishing myself. Creating chaos and punishment and self-harming behavior. Why?

For a long time, I didn't realize that I had other options in certain aspects of my life.

Because I was raised to win.

Being a competitor was my identity, and in some ways it still is. What's changed is that my desire for personal success has transformed into a desire for my clients' success—and I work towards that goal with a new kind of healthy intensity. However, that intensity nearly killed me. Because, when you are raised to win, you strive for the goal—whatever that goal might be. And if someone with power keeps moving the goalpost, or refusing to put points on the board when you score, that can be a very frustrating place indeed.

If I didn't win, my protector parts rushed to my defense with this thought: "You didn't win! But you are a winner! So, here's some new logic: if you don't win, you aren't worth anything."

I was frustrated and—inside my mind—worthless.

It was as if I had emotional sepsis.

Sepsis is a real physical condition that happens when your body experiences a traumatic event. The Mayo Clinic says it's the body's improper response to an infection. Events (like a serious wound or injury) can also trigger the condition, as the body tries to respond to a trauma. In advanced cases of sepsis, you can experience organ failure, blood poisoning, and all kinds of horrible complications.

The crazy thing is that our bodies all have the capacity to go into what is called "septic shock" if triggered by some form of bacterial infection (or other cause). Notice that sepsis is not an external disease, although it might be triggered by one. Sepsis is an internal response— with often chaotic and unpredictable results.

In the United States, someone is diagnosed with sepsis every 20 seconds.

Jim Henson, the creator of the Muppets, was battling a sore throat—he thought it was walking pneumonia. Things progressed quickly, and he had trouble breathing. He was rushed to a hospital to get a handle on the infection, according to accounts. Four days later, the creator of Kermit the Frog was dead—a result of sepsis and organ failure—his body's reaction to his symptoms.

When I played water polo, I wasn't afraid to fight. That was my reaction to competition, when the situation called for it. Not unlike hockey or other contact sports, aggressive behavior is part of the game. But the game of life (and work) is different. And, in the calm light of day, we all know that violence is not the answer. Especially when it comes to workplace conflict, disagreement, personal space, and mutual respect. Emotional sepsis can have severe consequences. Organ failure becomes organizational failure.

Yet, when our protector parts take over, we quite literally lose ourselves. We turn to base instincts, seeing life as a fierce competition where pushing people around (or screaming or demeaning or threatening) seems like the best and only option.

But it's not.

So, how can you find calm in the middle of the storm? How can you find some self-control when those around you are "losing it?" Or maybe, when you are?

Here's how to access new possibilities:

1. **"That's just how I am" isn't**—clients come to me all the time, and they say, "That's just how I am, Rob. I am a perfectionist," or "I am a competitor." As a coach, I can relate—I can say, "Me, too!" to both of those things. And I do. But what I remind them is that perfectionism or competitiveness is not an identity, it's a choice. These characteristics are a *part* of who you are. It's not you. Are you making a part of you into an identity? Are you trying to turn a part into a whole, forgetting yourself (your true Self) in the process?

2. **You Never Lose the Will to Win**—sometimes clients worry that coaching will cause them to "lose their edge" or somehow weaken their desire to achieve. The misunderstanding seems to show up as a resistance to being more compassionate (either to themselves or to the people around them), because caring is seen as a sign of weakness (a false belief). After all, we have to be hard on ourselves if we want to achieve, right? Wrong. You never lose the will to win; you just play the game a little differently. You can work 80 hours a week, berating your team and basically beating the shit out of people. But know that when you are berating others, you are ultimately berating yourself. There's a part of you that's saying, "You aren't good enough! You don't try hard enough! You are worthless!" so you spray that emotion at others. How's that working for you? For your team? When a client was feeling shitty about herself, her misdirected parts would say, "Go yell at somebody—like your subordinate, Sheila! I feel shitty, thanks to what my parts are telling me, but let me bully Sheila and pressure her—because now I'm letting it out! Yay, me—I'm not as bad as Sheila!"

    No, I had to tell my client: you're actually worse. How about if you silence that destructive part inside your head? To say that more plainly, how about recognizing that a part of you is not all of you, and never can be? The fact is, nobody works well under pressure and discouragement. Believe me, I've competed at the highest levels globally—and if you give in to the pressure, your parts come to your rescue.

    Those parts, although well-intentioned, will steal your focus in the big game! You want to bring your whole Self—your full Self—to tough situations. You don't have to show up inside a pressure-cooker, even if (and especially if!) the pressure is on. Notice that a little compassion goes a long way. When you aren't on your mind, you're really in the game. Compassion can help settle down that part of you that's robbing you of your ability to perform at your best.

3. **Notice the Feeling**—when it comes to working with tools at work, you have to get a feel for the new devices. Whether that's a new software platform at your architecture firm, or learning how to work with the steering-wheel clutch on the new forklift, you have to get a feel for it, right? When your parts are trying to take over, where does that feeling live inside you? For me, when the stress or anxiety part starts to rise up, I feel it in my solar plexus. I literally feel it in my chest. Imagine the experience when you were yelling at your team, or really tearing into Sheila, I asked my client. Where do you physically feel that memory? Where does it show up in your body? Does your face feel hot? Are your shoulders tense? There's no right or wrong answer here—the exercise is about awareness (for my client, and for you). Note the feeling, and speak it out loud. Awareness is the first step. What if, next time that tension or heat or tightness shows up, you see it for what it is? And you see, from a place of understanding, that you can choose differently. Yelling is one option, but as your coach I have to wonder: what else you got? The possibilities are limitless, and your job is to find a new possibility. Otherwise, you're just going to keep showing up the same way and expecting different results. And that, dear reader, is the definition of insanity. As you notice the sensation that emotions can have on your body, notice this fact as well: you can choose how you respond. Just because a train of thought shows up, doesn't mean you have to ride that train.

In sports, there's never just one way to win. The path to the goal is never fixed, even when you are running a play you have practiced 1,000 times. Life, like an opposing team, is always there—asking you, "Whatcha gonna do now?" Luckily, your personality and your response is never set in stone. Your psychology is yours to explore, just as you explore the many ways to win inside of a game. Whether that's tennis, baseball, or the game of life, you have the capacity to choose. To change. And, in order to help access that change, I've discovered that a quiet mind can really help.

I'm not sure if meditation has been something that has been useful to you. The comedian, Hannah Einbender, does a hilarious bit about how her ADHD brain responds to meditation. In her MAX special, she delivers this story with a light show and ear-splitting loud music, to signify that lack of quiet that rages inside her mind.

While you may not have a light show inside your head, I recognize that meditation may not be for everyone. But if you're willing to explore the power inside a quiet mind, and want to consider the opposite of pressure, I invite you to take a listen to this free audio: www.robkalwarowsky.com/chaos

Meditation, in particular guided meditation, has made a huge difference for me—and for my clients. It turns out that the noise inside my mind isn't the best of me. But it wasn't until I saw beyond the competitiveness, the cacophony and the catastrophe of life (it wasn't catastrophic, despite what my parts were feeling) I showed up differently. Maybe you will, too. Meditation, for me, can reveal the order inside the chaos.

It has been said that violence never solves anything. Turning to violence inevitably results in self-harm. Not self-care. Cruelty to yourself or to others is not a solution for success. Arrogance is the misunderstanding that makes us believe our frightened protector parts have earned the right to take control, and to let us lash out. But if you know anything about self-leadership by now, you know that you have to bring your whole Self (not just your parts) to the party.

Violence is not the antidote for anything. It's a poison for everything.

BREAKDOWN TO BREAK THROUGH

1. Functioning with intensity, in the pursuit of excellence, doesn't require violence. If you or someone you know is facing domestic abuse, help is available. The National Domestic Abuse Hotline in the USA is 800-799-7233, or you can text BEGIN to 88788.
2. Having a will to win is a great skill for success and the pursuit of excellence. But letting that desire turn into violence is first-class asshole boss behavior.
3. Violence is like an emotional sepsis—a poison where the antidote is always available. If you struggle with violent behavior, consider enrolling in an anger management program, therapy, or working with a coach, before the situation becomes worse.

EXPLORATIONS

1. What makes you really angry? What have you learned about anger, for yourself, and how do you respond when situations don't go your way?
2. Professional success and self-control don't always go together. Many sports teams and political leaders can exhibit flashes of anger. When is anger justified? What's the most effective way to use anger, and what is our angry behavior really trying to tell us? What underlying emotions is your anger masking?
3. Emotions are simply "energy in motion," at a basic level. Our emotions are expressions of our feelings. Considering your feelings on any given topic or person, where do those feelings come from? How can we acknowledge our feelings and separate our feelings from our behaviors—especially when those behaviors do not help us in our work or relationships?
4. Reflecting on past experiences, have you observed any patterns where someone's emotional outbursts or lack of emotional control

affected your work or personal life? How did this behavior influence your perception of them and your responses?

CHAPTER 6

THE ABUSIVE NARCISSIST

"Until the lions have their say, the tales of the hunt shall always glorify the hunter."

— CHINUA ACHEBE, NIGERIAN NOVELIST AND ESSAYIST, IN THE ART OF FICTION

"I am no longer accepting the things I cannot change. I am changing the things I cannot accept."

— ANGELA Y. DAVIS, AMERICAN POLITICAL ACTIVIST AND PHILOSOPHER

What's the difference between being selfish, self-centered, and a full-blown narcissist? Typically, it's a question of degree.

In the corporate world, narcissistic tendencies are often rewarded. Narcissists perform well in work environments—they frequently rise up to the highest levels. That's why, in the Swedish study, 1 in 5 people report having worked with or for this kind of self-centered person.

So is narcissism a function of success? Or something to be avoided, corrected and corralled? Are we exploring an essential characteristic for leadership, or a dangerous set of behaviors that can rob your team and your organization of engagement, efficiency and collaboration?

Let me be clear: toxic behaviors are something to understand, and avoid, not admire. Capitalizing on chaos begins with looking at the sources of workplace malfunction.

I have a part of me that can be an abusive narcissist, in moments. Anger and selfishness are a part of us all. The challenge starts when narcissistic parts take over, and over-index on situations (and people) with disastrous results.

Empathy is what separates a selfish person from a narcissist. That's according to Robert Taibbi, LCSW, a therapist and author based in Charlottesville, Virginia.

Taibbi says that self-centered people still have the capacity to be empathetic. For narcissists, they "see others as pawns. Narcissists often feel special, as if rules don't apply to them."

> *Right out of the gate, here's a quick test for narcissism: Do you have any colleagues, board members, and/or investors who view themselves as superior to others?*

From a perspective of selfishness, lack of empathy is where the narcissist stands out. If a true narcissist is being empathetic, Tiabbi says, they are faking it.

Dr. Joni Johnston is a clinical and forensic psychologist who has identified many narcissists in her work within the criminal justice system. She explains the key characteristics that define narcissists in *Psychology Today.*

For someone to be diagnosed with narcissistic personality disorder, Dr. Johnston says, they must meet at least five of these criteria:

Grandiosity. "I am better than everyone else, and other people are lucky to be around me."

Preoccupation with fantasies of success and power. "I live in a fantasy where I exaggerate my accomplishments and relationships to myself and others."

A feeling of being unique. "Because I am so special, I can only be understood by other special people. I want and deserve to be around high-status people, places, and things."

Requirement of excess admiration. "I want relationships where I am the center of attention, and you shower me with praise, attention, and loyalty. Stop doing this, and you have betrayed me."

Sense of entitlement. "I don't have to earn special treatment; I deserve it." Taibbi says that self-centered people have clear moral values, and can express regret over something as simple as cutting in line. Or as troubling as cheating on a partner. The narcissist, according to Taibbi, feels special: rules don't apply to them.

Interpersonally exploitative. "I have no problem using people to meet my own needs. Sometimes it's malicious, and sometimes it's because I can't even see that you have them." Taibbi takes it a step further: the narcissist will blame others for their own actions, as a way of deflecting criticism.

Lack of empathy. "You are responsible for my feelings, but I don't care about yours."

Envious of others. "I am threatened by people who have something I don't and look for ways to knock them down a peg or two."

Being arrogant and domineering. "Challenge me, criticize me, or ignore my needs, and I will find ways to pay you back–with contempt, criticism, insults, or threats."

Do any of these sound familiar? You may be working with a narcissist—or at the very least, someone with narcissistic tendencies. "Despite its overuse," Johnston writes, "narcissistic personality disorder [NPD] is rare. Studies have found that approximately 1% of the population meets the criteria," and qualify fully for the diagnosis. Other sources note that "among senior executives, that rate climbs to 3-5%."

And if you find that these characteristics describe yourself, you're not truly a full-blown narcissist. Because self-reflection and self-awareness are not part of the narcissist's playbook. A narcissist, when confronted with facts of their behavior, will more likely remind you that how they are is your fault. Or God's gift. You decide.

In the workplace, the people who suffer most from NPD (narcissistic personality disorder) aren't the folks who over-index on the selfishness scale. It's the people who work for these bosses.

THE FOUR TYPES OF NARCISSISTS

According to Los Angeles-based mental health expert, Dr. Ramani Durvasala, there are four types of narcissists that we can encounter in the workplace. She's the author of *Should I Stay or Should I Go: Surviving a Relationship with a Narcissist,* and one of the foremost authorities on the pitfalls and pains of dealing with narcissism. Which one(s) have you encountered at work?

1. **The Grandiose Narcissist:** arrogant, egotistical, attention-grabbing, validation-seeking, and unable to listen. That's the classical narcissist—lacking in empathy and only focused on themselves, in the never-ending pursuit of attention.

2. **The Malignant Narcissist:** Ramani says this person has all the characteristics of the grandiose narcissist, but they take it up a notch. These folks are also "really mean," she shares. "They will do bad things." When asked to elaborate, she refers to a Bernie Madoff type: someone who will embezzle a company, cheat on a partner, lie, and more. "They make great criminals," she explains. But they aren't sociopaths. "They might feel bad about hurting their family. But they often won't care about other victims."

3. **The Covert Narcissist:** that's someone who is put upon by the world, in a grandiose and self-serving way. "They say things like, 'Yeah, I'm a really great photographer, but the world never really noticed my greatness." These folks feel like "life has done them wrong," and they can often present, in a clinical setting,

as depressed and passive-aggressive. The covert narcissist wonders why the world doesn't see how great they are, while they practice blamestorming everyone and everything for their circumstances.

4. **The Communal Narcissist:** "I'm off to feed the homeless today," the communal narcissist explains, often littering the internet with all the good they do for others. However, underneath the broadcast messages of "giving back," there's a disconnect. They lack true empathy for the people they are trying to help, according to Dr. Ramani. And they need a lot of recognition for their "greatness" and "good works." "I often say, 'do good quietly,'" Ramani explains.

BUT CAN A NARCISSIST EVER CHANGE?

While change is always possible, the harder question for the narcissist is, "Do they really want to?" Without desire, progress is prohibited. Parts can take over the whole.

Pro tip: if you're trying to figure out how to do something, ask yourself if you really *want to*, first of all. Desire drives the whole show. Without want-to, the "how to" doesn't matter much.

For someone who is arrogant, self-focused, grandiose, and unapologetically self-absorbed, how is it in their best interest to change? What would that look like?

Kabir came into my leadership training program. From the start, he wanted to leave.

He's a high-level guy, very bright, very focused on his career. He leads digital transformation at a telecom company whose name you would immediately recognize.

And he wanted out the minute he got into my coaching program.

Because my leadership group was not "executive" enough for him. He knew all this leadership stuff already, he said, so there was nothing new to discover. On our first call, he blasted the group for being beneath him—and made it clear that I didn't have anything new to teach him. His attitude was: these folks on this call are not helping me get ahead, and neither are you.

Notice the narcissist is often unable to see (or care about) the repercussions of spraying that kind of condescending nonsense into a group of co-workers. Of course, if a narcissist cared about what you thought, they wouldn't be a narcissist.

Not surprisingly, some of his co-workers felt diminished and dismissed by Kabir—not just in the coaching program, but in their day-to-day experience of the guy. Some key employees had a conversation that went all the way to the CTO's office. When that conversation came back down to Kabir, it was like a bomb of chaos had been dropped on his head.

The conversation touched on things like disrespect. Fairness. Being demanding versus being effective. Kabir, a hard-charging guy who cared about his career (and still does) was facing a crossroads.

The company was not going to tolerate this kind of behavior. Unlike many organizations, this organization was not going to condone or support toxic leadership—and they called Kabir into account.

In this make-it-or-break-it career moment, Kabir found a way to do what most narcissists can't… or won't.

He listened.

After that meeting, we had a one-on-one call. Kabir seemed flushed. Flustered. Was he sweating?

"What's going on?" I asked him.

The dam burst. "All this shit happened," he explained, "and it's not my fault! It's nothing that I did," he protested, the words pouring out of him like a waterfall.

I listened.

I heard the deflection, the blame, the absence of regret. I gave him the space he needed to sort things out. When he arrived at silence, a new idea emerged.

Kabir accessed another skill that narcissists rarely possess: healthy self-awareness.

"I have to…" he said, his voice drifting off.

Where was he headed? I didn't move. Didn't speak. He exhaled, almost a sigh—he was letting go of something, but I wasn't sure what.

He rubbed the back of his neck. Looked at the ceiling to find his next thought. The word came from a deep place of realization. "Change," he said.

"I have to change… in order to survive."

Marshall Goldsmith wrote a great book, entitled *What Got You Here Won't Get You There.* Kabir was bringing that title to life, right before my eyes. Inside the chaos, he found something new—a new possibility emerged.

He could keep going, but he'd be working somewhere else—most likely bringing his bad habits with him. But he decided to make a different choice.

The narcissistic behaviors that had propelled Kabir to an elite level within the organization were the exact behaviors that had put his career on the chopping block.

On my end, a new person started to show up. The part of him that was creating chaos and challenge seemed to recede—rejoining the whole, as Kabir got in touch with his true Self. He began to trust his instincts, not just his insecurities. The arrogance and defensiveness seemed to subside. But for how long, I wondered?

As our work progressed, I reflected on the feedback I had received from his team and his co-workers. They used words that no one ever uses to describe a narcissist. Words like caring. Compassionate. The big phrase for me was, "He is so different."

If you want to know if a narcissist has changed, don't ask them— you might not get a straight answer. Ask the people around them.

True narcissists don't have a way to look at themselves and say, "I need to be different"—because their *modus operandi* is "You need to change." As a coach, a simple response comes to mind: "Is that true?"

Not just true because you say so—but true because it is so. Kabir saw his situation, and himself, from a new perspective.

Consider how the narcissist personality type is treated at your company. When narcissistic behaviors are rewarded, what's the motivation to do anything differently? Perhaps upper management needs to recognize that abusive supervision is a cancer that eats away at the organization.

"Dark leaders" can be hostile, abusive, and even Machiavellian (controlling and manipulative) in their behavior. A study in 2006 showed that abusive supervision costs US companies nearly $24 billion annually—measured in lost productivity, absenteeism, and health care costs. If you're wondering what those costs are now, consider: can your organization afford to pay the price, no matter what that current price may be?

A scientific study from the University of Quebec shows that *"the sustained display of hostile verbal and nonverbal behaviors"* can damage organizations in the following ways:

1. Lower job and life satisfaction
2. Lower commitment to the organization
3. Higher work-family conflict
4. Overall psychological distress
5. Lower employee creativity
6. Lower employee performance

If you care about employee productivity, employee engagement, and job satisfaction, why not take steps to move past the chaos?

We all know that there's a correlation between social dominance behaviors (valuing social hierarchy, self-interest, status, and power) and abusive supervision (another way of saying, "narcissistic leadership"). Toxic leaders don't have to be tolerated. Or indulged.

People (and organizations) can change—if they want to.

Kabir is living proof that the psychological part does not define the whole. Kabir, like a lot of high-performing narcissists, had a strong protector part—trying hard to protect him from the "harmful rays of self-reflection." The protector was over-indexing, pushing other people down, taking credit, avoiding blame by spraying it at others—you get the picture. But Kabir was lucky enough to work for a company that saw the value of coaching. Instead of tolerating toxicity or firing a talented (and misguided) employee, they invested. Invested in new ideas—so that Kabir had a chance to show up

Or he could leave.

He was presented with a choice. One way or the other, this was a choice for change. The chaos was too great. Kabir had a decision to make—and one way or the other, he was going to change.

Our coaching conversation provided the space for new ideas. New behaviors. And an understanding that the part can't keep running the whole show.

Kabir had to return to himself in a way that was healthy, even-handed, and confident. That way, he could show up differently for his team and his organization—because he didn't have anything to defend. Only opportunities to explore. And people to support.

What if your nearest narcissist doesn't face a moment of truth, like Kabir? It might be useful to explore what progress looks like, so that you (and your leadership team) can cultivate the change that's needed.

Nicole Arzt is a licensed family therapist based in Orange County, California. When working with dark leaders, the mantra of "trust but verify" is key, as one of the personality traits of a narcissist can be a tendency to say anything. Behavior observation and corroboration are crucial. Arzt offers six signs that a narcissist is open to change:

1. **The narcissist takes personal accountability:** Ownership, not blame, is what to look for here. Remember, talk is cheap—what actions are fulfilling the words?

2. **The narcissist listens to your feedback:** "I hear you" is a great start. But what, if anything, is done with the new message? What behaviors are people experiencing? Turning ideas into action—or providing even-handed feedback on what course

of action makes more sense—is the communication loop to look for here.

3. **The narcissist pays better attention to you and to others:** "Narcissists often have one-sided relationships. They spend time with people who value, prioritize or otherwise affirm their needs," Arzt shares. Is the narcissist surrounded by "Yes-men" (or -women), sycophants and ass-kissers? Or are new voices part of the conversation?

4. **The narcissist shows better emotional regulation skills:** Have you experienced an outburst of emotion from a narcissist? Rage, dramatics, tantrums, tears, and more must diminish in frequency and intensity. Feelings of entitlement don't show up as often (if at all).

5. **The narcissist authentically apologizes when slipping into old behaviors**: Remember the adage: actions speak louder than words. Notice if this is the first apology or the fourteenth. When behaviors change, apologies cease.

6. **The narcissist is consistent:** But in a good way! "A narcissist who wants to change will respect that connection and safety takes time. If they have hurt you in the past, they will know they need to earn back your trust. They won't rush you or become impatient if you're still cautious," Arzt shares.

If you find yourself working with a narcissist, communication is where progress begins—starting with the way you communicate with yourself. Dr. Durvasula, considered by many the leading authority on narcissistic relationships, and the author of *It's Not You* (The Open Field, 2024), says, "If you're going to stay in this relationship, you have to engage in something that I and others have called 'Radical Acceptance.'" Narcissists, she says, lack empathy—so seeing things from your perspective can be a flat-out impossibility. Can you accept that fact?

She explains that if you are dealing with a narcissist, don't defend. Don't engage. Don't explain. And don't personalize. These responses,

Dr. Durvasula says, will rob the narcissist of their power. And hopefully create some mental stability for you in the process.

Understand that setting strict boundaries is especially important. Just know that a narcissist is gonna step over them.

I had a client whose boss was a raging racist—unapologetic for slurs and often yelling at people. Of course, people spoke up and confronted the racist behavior. This asshole was reported to HR, and the company did an internal investigation. But the racist had a lot of power, so nothing happened. Nothing changed.

What would you do?

You can document everything. Identify the bad behavior. Set boundaries. Stop explaining. Start complaining. Have skip-level meetings. Take your story up the chain. Pray to the gods of HR, hoping they have the guts to do what's right.

But if your company won't invest in change, you have to *break the chain*. You have to break free from the chaos.

You have to remember the first rule of lifeguarding: *don't drown*. Is a narcissist trying to drown your company in a barrage of lies, blame, and disinformation?

See, if you are going to be useful to yourself or others, *don't drown*. You have to stay safe and sane, first and foremost.

Maybe, when working with a narcissist, what needs to change is you. What happens if you give yourself permission to disengage? No, you are not at fault (despite what you may have been told, or what the narcissist would like you to believe). Beyond the lies, you have to be true to yourself. Step out of the invalidating shadow, the dark clouds of blame and lies, and see who you really are.

After my TEDx talk, I got an email from a past client who was working for an abusive narcissist. She said, basically, "Great TEDx talk, love this stuff about narcissists… but what if you can't leave?"

It's easier said than done, but here is what I told her: You can leave.

As George Eliot famously said, "It's never too late to be who you might have been."

By the way, you know that George's real name was Mary Ann Evans, right? I'm guessing that she (he?) knew something about the subject of change.

You can change your circumstances, and you can change your life. That statement is not motivational; it's the way things work. The capacity for change is within you, right now, even if you (or your parts!) don't see it as a possibility. You can always change your circumstances, but first, you have to change your perspective. You have to see new possibilities—possibilities that the narcissist wants you to avoid!

I coached my client, the one who reached out after my talk. In our conversations, she came to see that she was not trapped. She had options. She had skills and talents that the narcissist had denied.

Not surprisingly, there was substantial evidence of her abilities, her innate value as a person—and her value to the organization. A value that she discovered would be more appreciated elsewhere, and now, people are constantly and consistently trying to hire her! She found a new career, and at first it wasn't easy. What made it easier?

The day she realized that *we* are the only thing we can change. And that change was in her power when she stopped giving it away to the abusive narcissist boss who was short-circuiting her career. Returning to Self, for her, revealed new options.

So, what can you do to keep yourself safe, and sane, when empathy is non-existent and mutual understanding is a bridge too far?

> "If you want to fly, you have to give up what weighs you down."
>
> — ROY T. BENNETT, THE LIGHT IN THE HEART

You may think that walking away—changing your role via an internal transfer, or changing your career via an external one—is a sign of defeat. But I see that choice as a sign of wisdom. Stepping back from one battle, so that you can fight another day, can be a long-term strategy for success.

It's almost impossible to "get ahead" when you work with a narcissist. They will take their success for themselves (more on that in the next chapter) and put the blame on you when you don't necessarily deserve it. That kind of treatment makes it tough to build a name for yourself. Not to mention the mental and emotional toll it can take regarding your self-worth.

Speak your truth, ask for what you need, share boundaries to let others know what you will and won't accept. But ultimately, if others can't hear and respect your truth, you know what you need to do.

And as I have said before, change may not be easy. But when others can't find new ways to behave, it's time for you to show yourself the empathy and compassion that the narcissist will never know. "Relationships with a narcissist are held in place by the hope of a 'someday better', with little evidence to support it will ever arrive," Dr. Durvasula says, in this interview with Lewis Howes. If something better doesn't arrive, does that mean it's time for you to leave?

Remember what it is that you want and what you value. Have you communicated clearly? Are you identifying self-centered behaviors in a way that's honest, objective, and clear? Don't get me wrong—I'm not blaming the victim here. But sometimes we can over-dramatize behavior, as well as limit our responses. That's not about being a victim; that's just being human. I've been there myself, where I needed an objective professional opinion in order to see things in a new way. I know from my own experience, on both sides of the coaching conversation, that a second set of eyes and ears always brings a new perspective to any situation. That point of view always has value, especially when dealing with a narcissist.

> *"Some of us think holding on makes us strong but sometimes it is letting go."*
>
> — HERMAN HESSE, NOBEL PRIZE-WINNING AUTHOR

Have you invested in coaching, so that you can make sure you are doing everything you can to create the life you want? When you are dealing with a narcissist, part of the drama is feeling that you are isolated and alone in your journey. With coaching, that's never the case—you don't have to go it alone.

With the narcissist, you may think you've tried everything. But what does a professional coach, focused on your success, have to say? That perspective may reinforce your own—or open up new possibilities that you haven't considered. Away from the toxic situation, in a moment of calm, consider: what do you want to achieve?

Of course, with coaching, there's only one way to find out. If you are curious to learn more about the power inside the coaching conversation, the best way to access it is (wait for it) via a coaching conversation. Does it make sense to set up a time to talk? Check out www.robkalwarowsky.com/chaos. New ideas are closer than you might think.

This meditation (www.robkalwarowsky.com/chaos) can help with finding some headspace to consider your options. Remember: sometimes you have to step away so that you can step forward. Breaking free from the narcissist's grip might be your best move yet.

BREAKDOWN TO BREAK THROUGH

1. **Prioritize Actions Over Words:** Focus on what the narcissist is doing rather than what they say. Genuine change is demonstrated through consistent actions, not just promises.
2. **Observe Reactions to Feedback:** Pay attention to whether the narcissist listens to and acts upon feedback. Effective communication involves turning ideas into actions and responding constructively to suggestions.

3. **Set and Enforce Boundaries:** Clearly define your limits and maintain them, knowing that narcissists may try to test or ignore them. Consistent boundaries are crucial for maintaining your well-being.

4. **Manage Your Emotional Response:** Avoid engaging in arguments or defending yourself, as this can empower the narcissist. Instead, focus on protecting your mental health and maintaining stability.

5. **Consider Professional Support:** Engage with a coach or therapist for guidance and support. Professional insights can help you navigate the challenges of dealing with narcissistic behavior and develop effective strategies.

EXPLORATIONS

1. Can you share a time when you noticed someone, perhaps a fellow leader or colleague, who exhibited behaviors typical of narcissism, such as only surrounding themselves with people who affirm their needs or frequently making grandiose claims? How did this impact your interactions with them?

2. Have you ever encountered someone who seemed to respond positively to feedback initially but failed to make any meaningful changes in their behavior? What were the key signs that the feedback was not being acted upon?

3. What happens to trust when people are dealing with narcissistic behavior? Do you believe a narcissist can change? Have you ever experienced a narcissist who proclaimed that they would change, or improve, or accept accountability... but they didn't?

4. Think of a situation where you had to set boundaries with someone who tested or ignored them. How did you enforce these boundaries, and what strategies did you find effective in maintaining your personal space and well-being?

CHAPTER 7

THE HIDDEN CHAOS

"Honesty is hardly ever heard. And mostly what I need from you. "

— BILLY JOEL, AMERICAN SONGWRITER, HONESTY

"I am no longer accepting the things I cannot change. I am changing the things I cannot accept."

— ANGELA Y. DAVIS, AMERICAN POLITICAL ACTIVIST AND PHILOSOPHER

Passive-aggressive bosses are always playing a game of charades. They are working super-hard to let you know what it is that they are upset about, without telling you directly. Their actions may be subtle, or overt, but the one thing the passive-aggressive boss will never do is tell you the truth.

I came into work on a Monday morning. The day was like any other. I had been at a client site the entire week before, so I came into the office at 7:45 am to grab a cup of coffee and chat with some of my co-workers. Simon, my manager, came into the break room with some news.

"Hey Rob," he said, "we gotta go see Celina in HR." I looked up from my coffee mug and saw that his brow was furrowed, like he was in some kind of pain.

Simon's eyes were darting back and forth. He was looking around the room as I got up to join him. *Why is he so jumpy?* I wondered.

He didn't seem like himself as we walked down to Celina's office. I didn't really know what was going on, but I sat down in front of Celina with Simon on my left. "I don't really know a good way to say this, Rob," she said.

"What's up?" I asked.

Celina told me about how my performance had been suffering. This information was news to me, as I had been working with clients onsite and busting my ass to do my job. Nothing was "suffering," other than me as I listened to these false accusations. Where was this coming from, and where was this headed?

Celina said that there was a bunch of work that had been left undone. This remark was news to me. And fake news, at that.

We began to play a game of "Gotcha."

Have you ever played "Gotcha?" It's a game where you scramble and run around and defend your hard work. Meanwhile, as you are trying to find the real objective, or "the ball," or the goal posts inside of a chaotic conversation where nothing makes sense. Then a senior leader starts throwing sticks in your spokes and putting you in the penalty box—sometimes, all at the same time. The real objective is always hidden, and the goal keeps shifting around.

While you are defending yourself, someone in management yells, "Gotcha!"

And then, you lose. It's not a fun game, because you are fighting an enemy you can't see. The rules are based on chaos—and they change to suit the needs of the person in charge.

"I've been on client sites for 40% of the year," I explained to Celina. "The rest of the time I was doing work for the clients—and the work was getting done. So, what's the real issue?"

Her answer surprised me. Turns out, I was identified as someone who is "not on the bus."

A great way to confuse the players in a game of "Gotcha!" is to make up a metaphor and expect them to understand it.

"Not on the bus?" What bus?

I didn't work for Greyhound (the bus company). My company didn't make me travel on a bus. So what, exactly, was she talking about?

You probably already know that there was no bus. Our CEO had hired a leadership coach, who had introduced this "get people on the bus" idea. It's a metaphor used for the evaluation of staff. The coach encouraged the CEO to evaluate people on a quarterly basis, deciding who was "on the bus" (performing well) versus "not on the bus." It's sort of a corporate version of *Survivor*, where you get voted off the island—or kicked off the bus. Luckily for me, I wasn't being fired. At least, as far as I could tell.

However, the CEO was playing a dangerous game. She was creating an "us versus them" culture by following the (horrible) advice of her coach. She wanted people to evaluate their team based on this "on the bus/off the bus" mentality. The end result?

Management started throwing people under the bus.

That's where I came into the story—when Carl decided to throw me under the bus.

Carl was a friend, I thought. He was head of the lab—our research and development department. Carl was nice to me. We would chat over coffee. Sometimes I would ask him about experiments (a big part of our work in heavy industry). He always took time to answer my questions. I never had anything bad to say about this guy. But there was one thing I didn't know about Carl.

He was a passive-aggressive asshole.

Carl was telling everyone—including Celina in HR—that I wasn't doing my job. Carl was trying to save his job and his department. A part of him reasoned that the way to save his headcount was to get rid of people in other departments. And when I say "people," I mean me.

He needed me to be the scapegoat for poor execution, so that he could somehow preserve his own team, so he made up a story about my work.

Remember, Simon was my boss. Carl wasn't even my supervisor! How could he possibly know my work quality or my performance? He couldn't—and he didn't.

Notice the first rule of being passive-aggressive: you don't talk about the problem with the person. You talk to everyone else. Your only action is behind-the-back. You go around the person you want to throw under the bus by saying, "This person is not on the bus." The passive-aggressive player either lies to your face or never speaks a word to the person who is at the heart of the situation.

And that hidden poison created a difficult situation for me.

I was able to bite my tongue and listen to these lies in Celina's office. I left, reprimanded and punished for a crime I didn't commit. Gotcha!

I survived for another eight months, until the game was on again. I was teaching a class, onsite, on a Monday morning. My boss came in and interrupted me. "Rob," he said, calmly, "we gotta go and talk to HR."

I didn't want to play Gotcha!, but I had to. This time, I was fired.

Who pulls a trainer out of a class to do something like that?

Harvard Business Review calls it "The Passive-Aggressive Organization."

The company had assumed a passive-aggressive stance, and it harmed the entire organization. The company's culture went down the toilet. In the end, I was the one who won this game of "Gotcha!"—because I wasn't going to let a bunch of lies cheat me out of being who I am. You may think it sounds crazy to try and play a game where the rules keep changing, the goals keep shifting, and lies are taken as fact. Guess what? You are right. How can you win inside of chaos?

So let me move to what you can do, right now, to address these passive-aggressive issues (and the people who perpetrate them).

Communication is the key.

Amy Gallo is the author of *Getting Along: How to Work with Anyone (Even Difficult People)*. She explains that passive-aggressive people are not forthcoming about what they are truly thinking. "They use indirect methods to convey their thoughts or feelings," she says.

You may be thinking that accountability is key when dealing with passive-aggressive people—and you're not wrong. But the *real* key—and it's more powerful than accountability, which can often feel one-sided with the passive-aggressive asshole—is *agreement*.

Holding someone accountable can mean calling them on the carpet, asking them to live by their words. Which is scary for someone who is passive aggressive. Especially if you make the mistake of calling them passive-aggressive. Chances are good that this label will make a person angry and defensive, not receptive to change.

Accountability is a delicate tool, not a blunt instrument. And it's not a label-maker. So, avoid spraying labels and calling it "effective communication." Don't label someone else's feelings. Focusing on agreement or accountability can feel like an accusation (for the passive-aggressive person) and something to defend, deflect, or deny. Mutual agreement is the key to accountability.

The best conversation starts with curiosity. I use a simple phrase, after I identify a behavior that's troubling me: "Tell me more—What's going on?"

The key is not the words in the phrase, but the intention behind the words. In my experience, the intention that works best is a sincere curiosity. After all, if you are saying, "*What's going on?*" but with a tone that says, "*Why are you such an insufferable douchebag?*" then you are being passive-aggressive!

Don't let a shield of false emotion steal your meaning. Recall the words from the Good Book: the truth shall set you free.

Be sincere, respectful, and authentic—give the behavior you wish to receive.

- "You said you would have the report done by Thursday. *Tell me more—What's going on?*"
- "Akush told me you weren't happy with my slides, especially the R&D piece. *Tell me more—What's going on?*"
- "Your last group email made me curious about your views on the team's goals. *Tell me more -what's going on?*

Whatever you do, take the convo off of Slack, WhatsApp, text, or email. Remove the keyboard from the conversation.

There are two reasons why:

1. *Written communication does not convey tone*—Slack and other written tools are the hideout of the passive-aggressive jackals in your organization. Hiding beyond the written word, these keyboard warriors pass out snark and double-talk that can't be maintained in a real conversation (even a phone call). Don't give these passive-aggressive players a home court advantage. If someone is trash-talking you in email, keep your responses professional and short. Don't get lost in your interpretation of a tone that's just not there. Pick up the phone, jump on a video call.

2. *The truth can hide behind a keyboard*—like tone, true intentions can hide behind a keyboard. Passive-aggressive people can be keyboard warriors. Don't take the bait. Don't fall into the trap of replying in a way that doesn't serve you—stay away from labels, but stay curious about behaviors.

CURIOSITY, NOT CONFRONTATION

When you go to the passive-aggressive person, you want to set boundaries around what's appropriate and not appropriate. Just remember: the reason they are being passive-aggressive is an inability to confront something. It is possible to be firm—particular around boundaries, which deal with what you will and won't accept—without being confrontational. Here's how:

Start with curiosity, on your journey to agreement.

Agreement is the key to closing the loop on communication. Sure, you may want to confront the passive aggressive person and let them know that their behavior is making you scream. But that kind of self-expression is not productive. That kind of action would mean that your parts are responding to their parts, which is the exact opposite of bringing your best self (your whole Self) to work.

Remember that when you are talking about boundaries and behavior, you are talking about the behavior, not the person. When you speak of what's on your mind, the passive-aggressive person may get uncomfortable. Or say something that stretches the truth. Instead of calling the person a liar, focus on the behavior. You're not angry—you're looking for solutions. "It seems to me," you might say, "that there are some things that are not being said." That's one way to address the behavior. What is the most honest—and caring—thing you can say, right now, to cut through the passive-aggressive BS? Stay curious and look for solutions around the behavior. Because you know that it's not the person, it's their parts, causing the actions.

If you want to communicate more effectively, and find agreement inside of accountability, you have to understand where the passive-aggressive behavior is coming from.

Inside the passive-aggressive behavior is an insecure and frightened part that is presenting a failed logic argument. Logic arguments can look like "If this, then that." A failed logic argument, asserted by a part and leading to passive-aggressive behavior, is filled with fear. "If you say that, the world will disintegrate!" the part demands—seeing chaos where there is none. "Cushion that feedback! Hide that behavior! Don't enter into a confrontation! You can't tell her the truth! You can't be seen for who and how you really are!"

Common fears, like the fear of rejection, drive passive-aggressive behavior. Or it's not even a fear as much as it is a feeling of powerlessness.

There may be a bunch of reasons why someone might want to be indirect, since they feel that they can't really influence a decision. Or perhaps someone feels invisible inside a process, so why support it? Perhaps there is an element of the perfectionist at work—and if someone can't be perfect, why even try?

This kind of thinking leads to back-channels and back-stabbing. However, the answer is as simple as having the courage to have a conversation. And that conversation has to start with yourself.

Begin with permission. Give yourself permission to have the conversation with the passive-aggressive person. Remember that you have the ability to maintain curiosity over confrontation. Before you go over someone's head, go straight to them and ask them what's going on.

I can appreciate feeling powerless inside an interaction—as if someone else holds all the cards. The passive aggressive person feels that you can't handle the truth—or that they can't handle the blowback if they are really being honest with the people around them.

Consider my situation, in the HR office, playing that first game of Gotcha: if Carl really had a problem with my performance, why didn't he bring the issue to my attention directly? We spoke often. Why not share the truth? In this organization, for Carl, lies were the easy way out. He spoke to HR and started a series of events, designed to preserve his team—not address my performance (because there was nothing to address). Where are the lies, inside your organization? And how are you building trust, so that people can focus on what really matters—instead of playing a game of Gotcha?

From lies, bad behaviors flourish in response to imagined fears. And, in my experience, passive-aggressive behavior is often based on an inability or unwillingness to communicate—because the consequences are somehow more than what the part can bear.

The good news is: you are more than the sum of your parts. You are resilient. You have the ability to set context, develop agreements, and explain situations. You (and your co-workers) are actually antifragile. That's according to Nassim Taleb, the author of *Antifragility*. Contrary to popular belief, people are not teacups or wine glasses (fragile things that break easily).

People are resilient. Built to bounce back. Ready to hear the truth.

Imagine a passive-aggressive alarm clock that thinks you can't handle finding out that it's 5 a.m. and you need to get up. So, the passive-aggressive alarm clock might tell your co-workers that it's early, but it won't communicate with you. So your alarm never rings.

How are you supposed to react when you don't have the true details? Maybe you don't like having your alarm go off at 5 a.m.—but if you've got an early meeting, or an early flight, you've got to handle the truth! And a little discomfort isn't going to break you, like a wine glass. What if your passive-aggressive alarm clock decides to "spare your feelings?" This clock of chaos will hide the truth. Your alarm clock appears to underestimate you, making decisions about what you can and can't handle.

Are you treating your team the same way? Who are you underestimating? Who is underestimating you? Perhaps a clear dialogue around the importance of real-time and relevant information is in order.

The passive aggressive part is trapped in a misunderstanding around what people can and can't handle. And probably, a misunderstanding around what they can handle themselves. I'm talking about dealing with the truth. Being straightforward inside of communication, action and collaboration, is key to a healthy organization.

What happens when we see that people are resilient—even anti-fragile? What happens when we see that our parts are over-indexing on a misunderstanding? "I can't tell her what's really on my mind," for example. Is that a fact—or perhaps an opportunity for some coaching, on a new kind of conversation? Is it easier to underestimate people and try to control their responses because we lack the communication skills to really express ourselves?

Kim Scott is the author of *Radical Candor*. In her book, she talks about *kind, clear, specific and sincere* communication. She calls passive aggressive behavior *ruinous empathy*—where you try to spare someone's feelings, so you don't tell them what they need to know.

When my company let me go, the company did me a favor. They finally told me what I needed to know. I learned many valuable lessons on my way out—and now, I help others to make sure that passive aggressive assholes don't ruin their day (or their careers). Acceptance—of our circumstances, of our parts, of our resilience—is the first step in healing. And understanding that yes, in fact, people can handle the truth.

To help get to a place where you can hear and share the truth, I recommend taking a moment for a breathing exercise. Center yourself before that difficult conversation to make sure that you are in a neutral place where curiosity and agreement can flow more easily. Find a private place where you can be undisturbed for 5 minutes (very doable) and take time to go through this short breathing exercise: www.robkalwarowsky.com/chaos.

BREAKDOWN TO BREAK THROUGH

Here are five ways to deal with passive-aggressive behavior.

1. **Engage Directly and Personally:** Avoid dealing with passive-aggressive issues through indirect communication or gossip. Address the person directly, focusing on specific behaviors rather than generalities or labels. Face-to-face conversations or video calls are more effective than written communication, which can mask true intentions.

2. **Use Sincere Curiosity:** When addressing passive-aggressive behavior, approach the conversation with genuine curiosity rather than confrontation. Use open-ended questions like "Tell me more – What's going on?" to encourage honest discussion and uncover underlying issues without making the other person defensive.

3. **Avoid Labels and Accusations:** Refrain from labeling someone as passive-aggressive or making accusations. Instead, focus

on describing the specific behavior and how it affects you. This approach minimizes defensiveness and helps maintain a constructive dialogue.

4. **Set Clear Boundaries:** Establish and communicate clear boundaries regarding acceptable behavior. Be firm but not confrontational, focusing on what is and isn't acceptable without attacking the person's character. This clarity helps manage expectations and reduce passive-aggressive behavior.

5. **Seek Agreement and Solutions:** Strive for mutual understanding and agreement on how to move forward. Emphasize finding solutions and reaching a common ground rather than engaging in a power struggle or focusing on past grievances. This approach fosters a collaborative environment and helps address the root causes of passive-aggressive behavior.

EXPLORATIONS

1. Have you ever found yourself playing a game of "Gotcha?" Who started it? Do you like it when a speaker, co-worker, or teacher throws out a question, and you know that it's the start of the Gotcha game?

2. Can you recall a specific instance when you encountered passive-aggressive behavior from a colleague or supervisor? How did their indirect communication affect the situation, and how did you respond? How did that situation impact your leadership style—what did you learn from it?

3. Have you ever noticed yourself displaying passive-aggressive behavior, such as speaking about someone behind their back or using indirect communication to express frustration? What triggered that behavior, and how did it impact your relationships?

4. Where does passive-aggressive behavior come from, and how often do you see it in your organization?

5. When dealing with someone who is being passive-aggressive, what strategies have you found effective in moving the conversation towards a more direct and open discussion? How do you avoid falling into passive-aggressive patterns yourself during such interactions?

6. How do you address passive-aggressive behavior without escalating into conflict?

CHAPTER 8

THE PASSIVE EGOCENTRIC PROBLEM

"Never allow someone to be your priority while allowing yourself to be their option. "

— MARK TWAIN, AUTHOR OF HUCKLEBERRY FINN AND TOM SAWYER

"Some people are like birds. You help them to fly and once they are in the air, they shit on you."

— UNKNOWN

Put your name on every slide," my mom told me.

She also said I needed to put my name on all the reports that I created.

On. Every. Page.

Was she going too far with the strategy, from when I went to camp? We got a sharpie and wrote my name in all my underwear. Still not sure why. Were there a lot of hidden underwear thieves in Ontario?

But when, as an adult, someone at work took my PowerPoint and put their name on it I remembered.

Mom always knows best.

When you are dealing with a passive egocentric person, they think nothing of taking credit for other folks' work. I don't know if they will take your underwear, but these assholes will absolutely deny you any notoriety. They prefer to keep it all for themselves. The passive egocentric problem creates chaos in the workplace on multiple levels. Have you worked within this environment?

You know if you're experiencing passive egocentric behavior when:

1. **Acknowledgement is absent:** Your boss/colleague/investor/board member refuses to acknowledge your contribution, and grabs all the glory for themselves.

2. **Gratitude goes on holiday:** They don't say thank you, or offer appreciation. Instead, they take credit for your work in a public forum.

3. **Public Deception:** The passive egocentric can't be gracious and give credit where credit is due (because the narcissist part thinks that they deserve all the credit). If they were grateful in private, but the tune changed in front of the group, online or in front of upper management, remember: insincere gratitude is passive egocentric behavior. You may feel ashamed, dismissed, neglected or invisible, as the passive egocentric will not identify you or your work in a public forum.

The sting of working with a passive egocentric is especially hurtful when you have done all of the work, and receive none of the credit. It's a sensation of being dismissed, of being stepped on while someone else uses your hard work to advance their agenda and their career.

In a word, working with a passive egocentric can make you feel used.

To be fair, employment in an organization allows the organization to use your talents and skills. In return, you are rewarded with compensation. That's how work works.

However, if you work for a passive egocentric, you are denied the credit for your work. When acknowledgement is withheld, you miss the opportunity to be recognized for your work. Why? Why does it have to be like this, in some organizations? In order to find the answer, we have to look inside the passive egocentric—and the parts that are running the show.

Inside the passive egocentric, there's a part of them that wants recognition. It's a manager-part that broadcasts a series of misunderstandings:

1. What's mine is mine and what's yours is mine, if it helps me to get what I want
2. Recognizing others diminishes me (actually, the exact opposite is true)
3. You are the boss, you don't owe anybody anything. Take what's given to you, claim it for yourself, and tell your own story!

The saddest part of this chapter might be this fact: passive egocentric narcissists (yes, it's a form of narcissism) are often promoted. They do a great job of stealing credit, and claiming work (whether they did it or not). Egocentric narcissists crave the spotlight, and hate to share it. And, for leaders who can't see past the bright footlights to find the truth, these assholes get promoted.

My client, Kevin, wasn't getting promoted. He was surrounded by people who had no shame around stealing the spotlight. And, as a side effect, laying blame. Because the same manager-part that craves credit fears responsibility—especially when they are responsible for poor performance.

But Kevin's performance wasn't poor. In fact, he was kinda crushing it. He was a division president at a Fortune 500 tech company. He had responsibility for about 1,000 employees! When I met him, via Zoom, the story that unfolded was sad and unfortunate—but fixable!

"I've been in the same job grade for six years," he began. "I don't get promoted. Yet I keep saving my company and my division, over and over again," he told me.

When he dove into the details, I realized he had saved his company an ungodly amount of money. He put together a solution that allows his team to see the expenses of somebody in San Francisco, for monthly expenditures on Microsoft Teams, for example. That may not sound like much, but that level of reporting detail and granularity exists inside a company with tens of thousands of employees! Kevin's work was incredible. But I had a question for him.

"How are you talking about yourself?" I asked.

Basically, he told me, he wasn't. He was frustrated that he hadn't been promoted, but he had never asked for a promotion! He had a belief system—and many of us do—that says, "I'm modest—I can't talk about myself." Is there a part of you that believes that last statement?

Many of my colleagues in Australia call it the "tall poppy syndrome". You don't want to stand up, and stand out, because then you will be the "tall poppy". And the tall poppy is the first thing to be cut down, an easy target for those who want to take you out.

But stepping out of the poppy field, there's a difference between bragging, sharing…and silence. Being so modest that you can't ask for what you want isn't a virtue, it's a hindrance. A part of you is keeping you from what you deserve. After all, if people don't know what you can do for them, and for the organization, how do people come to understand your value? And if people don't understand your value, how are you ever going to be paid what you are worth? Are you willing to be treated like a doormat, via your silence? If so, how can you ever expect to be promoted?

False modesty is still false.

And Kevin wasn't stealing credit for anyone else's work. His approach was silence—and that looked like a "solid work ethic" for him. He was simply needing to share his story—to let his own light shine, just a little bit.

The great acting teacher, Stella Adler, famously said, "You've got to have a talent, for your talent." If you don't share your story, how will anyone hear it?

Being told to be modest is an experience, for most of us, from childhood. "Don't be the tall poppy!" But that kind of guidance can activate a part of ourselves that over-indexes on keeping our mouths shut—even when it's time to speak up.

After all, if you only take what life gives you, you're going to get taken advantage of. I'm not advocating for anyone to become a passive egocentric asshole—I'm advocating for you to tell your story with honesty, and frequency. I'm advocating for the thing that the passive egocentric narcissist hates: open communication—and telling the truth.

WHAT SEPARATES HONEST COMMUNICATION FROM BRAGGING

There's what you say, and there's the way that you say it. If you are sharing your success from a place of narcissistic greed, it doesn't really matter what you say. People know and observe and respond to your parts, on an instinctual level. The way you show up creates the world around you. People see your agenda, no matter how hard your parts are working to hide it. Better to be honest, straightforward and clear—in your work and in your communication. That's how you show up, when your whole Self is available.

Make room for a conversation with that part of you that believes that *modesty is the best policy*. Because you know that the actual phrase is, "HONESTY is the best policy."

See, your parts don't know the best policy—but they think they do! And your parts don't know how to tell time. There are parts of you that still think you are seven years old. Your parts think that you are stuck in childhood and someone you respect is saying, "Don't be the tall poppy!" What part of you is scolding you for the past, right now? And how can you bring yourself back to the present? The past is fixed. We can't change it. We are who we are because of it, and in spite of it. But through it all: we all have the capacity to change (despite the fact that our parts can be reluctant to do so).

Our parts are caught. Trapped in time. Unable to get to the here and now, because they are responding to the then and there.

How's that gonna turn out?

If you can't see where you are, right now, how are you going to make a wise decision? What happened to you when you were 7, or when you were in the pandemic, or when you were in that last relationship…that's not here anymore. Even though your parts may believe that to be the case, it is not. The past reminds us, it does not define us.

SHARING AND SERVICE

It has been said that sharing is caring. And, when sharing is done from a place of service, it is caring. Caring for yourself (also called "self-care") and caring for your career—as well as helping the folks who you serve— is a return to Self. Kevin needed to see things as they are now, and understand that service means sharing. Otherwise, how do people come to understand your values, your talents, your abilities…and your goals?

After all, if you expect to be promoted and you haven't shared the reasons why that needs to happen, do you think it is realistic to expect that someone would magically see you in some deep and holistic way, and offer you the promotion of your dreams?

That's not how life works. We have a disconnect between wanting what we want (career advancement, financial success, relationships that matter) and wanting what our parts want (keep your mouth shut, you don't deserve better than this, stay silent so no one things you are bragging, meritocracy is real, people will see your magic and reward you for it, the list goes on). Can you hear the lies and misunderstandings? Yes, that's what I'm talking about. And what I started talking about with Kevin.

Our parts can get lost in the past, bringing historical perspectives to current events. While it's true that those who don't learn from history are often destined to repeat it, consider this history lesson: you are more than your past. In fact, the way that we access the past is only through memory—often a memory that triggers one of our parts to shield us from an imagined outcome. Instead of allowing our whole Self to deal with what is, we let our parts deprive us of real-time assessment. From a place of calm, relaxed trust, we return to the Self, instead of engaging a part that just doesn't see the real situation.

I worked with Kevin to help him reframe his communication. Rather than jumping in with a bunch of tactics ("hey, let's update your LinkedIn profile!") we started at a higher level. We created some space for greater trust, so that he could take whatever action made the most sense for him. In order to see all of his options, he had to come back to himself, noticing what his parts were saying but finding new ways of responding to the noise.

We worked to calm down the part of him that was afraid of what might happen if people knew how talented and innovative he really was. Kevin didn't like the self-promotional approach of many of his colleagues. He said it didn't feel right to him.

Can you imagine if I tried to coach him on a strategy to try and re-create somebody else's story, or implement tactics that worked for someone else? No. He needed to create a new kind of conversation around his contribution. And that wasn't going to come from someone else's ideas or maneuvers. His path forward, I knew, was inside of him—and that's where we began our coaching journey.

Our first step was permission.

He had to give himself permission to remind his parts that he was an adult, not a scared little boy. He needed to give himself permission to tell his own story. Permission to allow that story to be something other than bragging, sales or self-promotion. He needed to see the value inside the truth was greater than the punishment inside of silence.

Before he decided to blow up his LinkedIn profile or dump some personal-branding missile on his boss's desk, he needed some self-authorization. He needed to make it OK to access some greater wisdom and creativity, in order to open up to possibilities (instead of falling prey to someone else's template or tactics). Openness is key to accessing the whole self. He needed to come to terms with the parts that were trying to pull him into the past, unburdening himself of the ideas that were keeping him trapped.

Have you been there?

"Would it be ok with you…" I began, and we explored ways to foster trust between his parts and his true Self. In the final chapter, I'll share more on how this process can take place, for you and for your teams. But for now, suffice it to say: permission was the key.

When Kevin realized that he could share his story from a place of service, not self-promotion, his conversations started to change. When he gave himself permission to ask for what he wanted (instead of just accepting what he thought he could get), his career started to shift.

The process was gradual, as he took a methodical and step-by-step approach to making an impact. Here are the three key things that showed up for him, and they translated into new conversations around his career:

1. **He didn't have to "sell" himself**—Kevin's background, like mine, is in engineering. The idea of "selling himself" or trying to persuade others wasn't something that appealed to him. In fact, it didn't really make sense. But he understood how to engineer a solution. And he was adept at finding problems to solve. The thing that changed? After he found solutions and solved problems, he made sure that he shared his results across various divisions. He wasn't sharing because he wanted to sell himself into a new job—he was sharing so that the organization could see progress—and know more about the kind of service he could offer. The key shift was when he identified with the servant's heart—the spirit of servant leadership. In case you are curious, servant leadership was first coined in an essay by Robert Greenleaf, published in 1970. Consider this description of the servant leader, from the Greenleaf Institute:

   "The difference [in the servant leader] manifests itself in the care taken by the servant-first to make sure that other people's

highest priority needs are being served. The best test, and difficult to administer, is: Do those served grow as persons? Do they, while being served, become healthier, wiser, freer, more autonomous, more likely themselves to become servants? A servant-leader focuses primarily on the growth and well-being of people and the communities [corporations] to which they belong. While traditional leadership generally involves the accumulation and exercise of power by one at the "top of the pyramid," servant leadership is different. The servant-leader shares power, puts the needs of others first and helps people develop and perform as highly as possible. Servant leadership is the exact opposite of passive egocentric asshole behavior—and the solution to the passive egocentric problem.

2. **He realized his work didn't speak for itself**—Kevin quickly acknowledged that his company was not a pure meritocracy. In other words, people were not promoted for their hard work and accomplishments. There were other aspects at play, especially at his executive level—such as relationships, and a shared knowledge of what he wanted for his career. You can't assume that people know what you are working on, and what outcomes you are creating—or what ambitions you have inside of you. He started taking meetings—even informal ones, via Microsoft Teams—to build his relationships within the company. We worked together to identify conversational strategies—some talking points that, with the right permission, could be shared in the context of service. His work didn't speak for itself, so in the spirit of offering resources and capabilities, he learned to share what he had done. A key phrase for him was, "Could your division benefit from something like this?" and also, "I'd be glad to help you to create similar results, if you are interested." He wasn't sharing so that he could get applause, likes and followers—he was sharing so that the organization could be better.

3. **Rewards are the After-Effect of Good Communication:**
   Kevin started to see that he was being perceived differently.
   He didn't need to grab credit from others in order to share
   accomplishments—he took an even-handed approach that
   was gracious to his team. The difference was he was also gracious, and kind, to himself. Along the way, he experienced that
   honesty is not arrogance. He wasn't focused on a particular
   outcome, at first, other than honesty, sharing and service. But
   sure enough: new opportunities started finding him. After all,
   once people know what you can do, they often ask you to do
   more of it! Especially if what you are doing and creating is built
   on integrity, and comes from a place of servant leadership.

There's a right way to talk about yourself and your accomplishments. Unfortunately, the passive egocentric part won't allow for that
kind of dialogue. It's time to break that pattern, and erase that problem.

The key to thriving in this kind of environment, where people are
taking credit for your hard work, is to take some steps to be kind to
yourself. Here are four things you can do, and they build on Kevin's
example, to make sure that you do not fall victim to a passive egocentric person:

1. **Find Some Head Space**—you've got to take time to calm
   down, when you are confronted with passive egocentric behavior. You may want to call somebody out, right away—but that
   can be a big mistake. That's according to Brian Uzzi, a professor of leadership and organizational change at Northwestern
   University's Kellogg School of Management. "If you're emotionally piqued [a fancy way of saying, 'pissed off'] it's not the
   time to talk about it. Your mind is not working at its best and
   you might end up being out-argued," he says. Maybe, in ret-
   rospect, they did mention your name in the presentation more
   than you originally thought? Look, I'm not trying to soft-pedal
   being ignored. But a calm approach is the only one that works.

Get defensive, get angry, and you run the risk of making the situation worse. There's a way to have the conversation, and a clear-headed calm place is always best.

2. **How Bad Do You Need the Credit?**—it always hurts to be ignored when you have worked hard on a project. Believe me, I know! My asshole boss, Zeke—do you remember him from the previous chapter? He told me that his boss was thrilled with what I had put in "my report". To my face, he gave me credit for the work—which was all a puppet show, because Zeke had told me what to write! So not only was I pissed that he "congratulated" me for turning into a human typewriter for him, but also I know for a fact that he took credit for the report in front of his boss. What gave me some peace of mind was recognizing that I didn't need the credit for Zeke's hair-brained scheme and wild assertions. In fact, I was worried that people would associate my name with this half-assed report! Sometimes realizing that you don't need to win every battle can provide some comfort. But, if you find yourself saying, "Oh, well, that's just how it goes," while your boss continues to shit in your general direction…well, how's that working for you? Making your boss shine is often part of the gig—and you are there to make them look good. Hopefully, there's an appreciation for your contribution on the back end of those efforts. Then again, how much does recognition really matter, when your whole Self answers that question?

3. **Boundaries are Big**—as I mentioned in the previous chapter, setting boundaries around a project or task can be a big help. If you suspect that someone is going take credit for your work, have a calm conversation to establish some boundaries. Look in the direction of agreement, and ask for the recognition you deserve (if the project goes well). Just understand that this recognition can cut both ways, if the work is not on time or on budget! Come what may, you have a shared understanding and

an agreement around how recognition is going to be shared—especially when there may be compensation involved. But even when money isn't at stake, there's still value in setting boundaries and making sure that your work is not stolen, obscured or forgotten.

4. **Standing Up For Yourself Doesn't Make You a Tall Poppy—** if you are the victim of blame at work—being recognized in a way that's not fair—you have two choices. Stay silent and take it, or speak up and change it. My sincere hope is that you will speak up for yourself, and speak out against any kind of falsehood or misrepresentation of your work. Just consider *how* that conversation needs to take place. Because confronting a passive egocentric person at the next team meeting, with 17 other people looking on via Zoom, is probably not the right approach. But neither is being mealy-mouthed, and staying silent. You teach people how to treat you, by the words that you choose. Take time to choose the words that will help you most, and that create the boundaries that create honesty for everyone.

In the *Harvard Business Review*, Uzzi advises asking questions instead of making accusations. That way, the passive egocentric person has an opportunity to explain why they felt justified in taking credit for the idea. Remember, just because a part of someone demonstrates passive egocentric behavior doesn't make them an asshole. Redemption and understanding could be as close as your next conversation.

"Research shows that it's much better to ask why it happened than to make a claim," says Uzzi. You say something like: *How did you feel the presentation went? Did you feel like you were able to hit all the main points?* You're trying to open up a dialogue—but don't make it a guessing game, when it comes to what you want to share. Because hiding the truth is passive aggressive! Come straight at it, Uzzi suggests: "*I noticed that when you talked about the project you said 'I' instead of 'we'.*

Was that intentional? Why did you present it that way?" The response can open the door to a dialogue about boundaries, expectations and ultimately, agreement. That way, you discover the antidote to passive egocentric behavior.

For so many of my clients, the key to new behavior starts with a conversation. A conversation that's internal, first of all. That way, the over-indexing parts can find some calm, peace and trust. From that kind of even-handed internal dialogue, your whole self comes into play—not just the parts that are overtaking the conversation. That internal dialogue is facilitated via the coaching conversation, including guided meditation. My experience has shown me that a neutral third-party resource can help you to find new internal resources.

Then, there is often a conversation that's external—addressing the passive egocentric behavior, so that new boundaries and behaviors can be established. It's very common that folks don't want to talk about themselves, and the impulse isn't without merit. Still, you have to share your story in order to let others know what you can do. The right approach is having that conversation from a place of servant leadership, without going over-the-top and taking someone else's work as your own.

BREAKDOWN TO BREAK THROUGH

Here are five takeaways for dealing with a passive-egocentric problem:

1. **Document Your Contributions:** Keep detailed records of your work and achievements. Ensure that you have evidence of your contributions, such as emails, reports, and presentations. This documentation can help you assert your role in projects and address any attempts by anyone to take undue credit.

2. **Communicate Your Achievements:** Proactively share your successes and contributions in a way that highlights your role without coming across as boastful. Regularly update your key stakeholders on your progress and achievements, making sure your contributions

are visible and recognized. A side effect is this strategy accelerates your career success.

3. **Address the Issue Directly:** If you feel someone is consistently taking credit for your work, consider having a direct but respectful conversation with them. Use phrases like, "I noticed that my contribution to the project wasn't mentioned during the meeting. Can we discuss how we can ensure that contributions are accurately recognized?"

4. **Find Calm Before Acting:** When faced with passive-egocentric behavior, take time to cool down before addressing the issue. Avoid immediate confrontation when you're emotionally charged, as it can lead to unproductive arguments. Instead, approach the situation calmly and thoughtfully to ensure a more effective resolution.

5. **Evaluate the Importance of Recognition:** Reflect on how crucial it is for you to receive recognition for your contributions. Sometimes, accepting that not every battle is worth fighting can provide comfort. However, if lack of acknowledgment is a recurring issue, assess its impact on your job satisfaction and career progression, and decide if it needs to be addressed.

6. **Set Clear Boundaries and Communicate Effectively:** Establish boundaries around credit and recognition for your work. Have a calm, clear conversation with the passive egocentric person to outline expectations for how contributions will be acknowledged. Use questions rather than accusations to open a dialogue about credit and recognition, and ensure there is a mutual understanding of how to handle such situations moving forward.

EXPLORATIONS

1. **Reflect on a time when you contributed significantly to a project** or task but felt that your work went unrecognized. What specific behaviors or actions led you to feel that your contributions were overlooked?

- How did the lack of recognition impact your motivation and job satisfaction?
- Did you observe any patterns in how credit was given or withheld in your workplace?
- What was your initial reaction, and how did you handle the situation?

2. **Talk it Out:** How can you communicate to ensure that your contributions are recognized? What steps can you take to effectively communicate your achievements and gain acknowledgment?

3. **What's really the big deal, if you don't get recognition?** Is that their issue, or yours?

4. **How do you recognize the contributions of your team?** As a leader, how often do you give recognition to your people? Do you adhere to the Vince Lombardi quote, "praise in public, criticize (punish) in private"?

CHAPTER 9

CLEANING UP THE CHAOS, WITH THE MESSY BOSS

> *"It is not the strongest of the species that survive, nor the most intelligent, but the one most responsive to change."*
>
> — CHARLES DARWIN, AUTHOR OF ORIGIN OF THE SPECIES AND FATHER OF THE THEORY OF EVOLUTION

> *"Even if you are on the right track, you'll get run over if you just sit there."*
>
> — WILL ROGERS, AMERICAN COWBOY HUMORIST AND ENTERTAINER

There's a big difference between uncertainty and indecisiveness. Uncertainty is all around us. No one can predict the future. Despite our best efforts, the past is history, and tomorrow is a mystery. Yet, in this world of uncertainty, from inside the chaos, we all have the ability to make decisions. We can always make choices.

But for messy bosses, making decisions is tricky. Sometimes, it's impossible. And the choices that messy bosses make can create challenges that you have to fix. Or overcome. Or perhaps just ignore?

I hate to say, "ignore," but unlike the other Destructive Six, the messy boss is actually kinda benign. Not especially dangerous to your career, but a nuisance nonetheless. A creator of chaos, whether intentional or not, is something that must be addressed.

Messy bosses aren't out to get you; they just don't know how to manage effectively.

For the messy boss, what most folks would call "good management" is elusive. Setting instructions, creating project plans, providing deadlines, establishing expectations… this kind of leader can't seem to get there. They are not actively destructive, but the inability to make a decision, and set a direction, causes challenges for everyone around them.

Most managers, and most messy bosses, would say that they are just trying their best. Perhaps they were the best engineer in the group, and now they are leading the team. Have they been trained in leadership? Effective communication? Dispute mediation? Scheduling? Strategy? Ah, details, details. There's also a difference between personal success and managerial support. If you've got a manager who hasn't been trained on how to lead others, you're not alone.

Harvard Business Review published a study of over 17,000 leaders worldwide. The average age of supervisors in the businesses represented was 33. But the average leadership training program didn't occur for leaders until they were 42.

That's a nine-year gap. Nine years of making mistakes and messes before receiving leadership training as a supervisor. What gives?

Management is making a mess, and it's due to a lack of training. "Practicing anything mildly important, like say skiing or golf, without training is inadvisable. The fact that so many of your managers are practicing leadership without training should alarm you," Jack Zenger says. He's the author of *Making Yourself Indispensable,* the CEO of Zenger/Folkman, and the author of the HBR article.

For messy bosses, there are some simple steps that can help correct the chaos. I know, because I've often run into one of the challenges that can cause folks to make a bit of a mess: going too fast.

I'm running 100 miles an hour, and when I delegate to my team or share instructions with the folks closest to me, I don't want to trip over the details. So, uh, well… sometimes I leave them out! Luckily, some self-awareness has helped me to overcome some natural tendencies. Combining this awareness with a great team, I have discovered how to avoid being a messy manager. Now I help others to do the same.

The first course-correction for the messy leader isn't really a mindset shift as much as it is an understanding issue: you have to understand what your people need. Here are four ways to make sure that you leave the mess and replace it with your best:

1. **Go Slow to Go Fast:** The problem with going too fast is that you can't help but miss the details. And the details matter when it comes to delegation. The first step in avoiding a mess? These two words: Slow down. Acceleration and growth inside an organization are like driving a race car, at times. Pushing the car too hard is going to cause a crash or engine failure.

    In her book, *Success from Anywhere,* Karen Mangia interviews Canadian race-car driver James Hinchcliffe. He explains how you have to slow down to go fast: "At 330 feet per second, inside a four-wheeled missile where you are pinned to your seat every time you make a left turn, the only way to respond to anything and everything is from a place of neutrality." The car may be in 11th gear, but you have to remain in neutral. Neutrality is the result when you don't let your parts take the wheel.

2. **The Critical Question:** No matter how fast you're moving, you have to keep your eye on what matters most. This single question can help guide you, reminding you of where you need to put your attention. "What needs to be done?" That question is useful for me personally, but also for my team. I want them to be able to see what needs to be done. Otherwise, we play a game of "Mother, May I?" where they have to ask me for

permission before they touch the keyboard, send the email, or book the appointment. That kind of micromanagement is not appealing! No thanks! I need leaders around me. And when I am decisive, I empower others to make decisions—recognizing the behavior that's a part of success and course-correcting when it's not. For me, what needs to be done is always an emphasis on the details when giving direction. At my best, I don't just give out random assignments, I provide clarity around the due date on a deliverable. I don't just need this random report, I need it by the end of the day on Thursday. Makes sense, right? But sometimes, running and gunning, I miss the details. That's why Step #3 is crucial.

3. **Stay Open to Feedback and Questions:** My fail-safe strategy is to always make sure that I close the loop with anyone I'm working with. That means making sure the message is received, whatever the message may be, as well as letting them know that they can always come to me with questions. That's not just lip service; I need to be available to offer clarification. "Ask me when you don't know," I say, "because my brain might be running a mile a minute and I left something out." Remember, you have to speak your team's language. You have to share your ideas and your initiatives and your direction and your guidance in a way that creates clarity.

Clarity is the key to avoiding a mess, so slow down. You're not delaying results, you are avoiding chaos and messes. Focus on what needs to be done. And stay open to feedback and questions.

What if you are on the receiving end of a messy boss, where details are scarce and direction is murky? Asking for clarification is key. "When's the deadline?" you may ask. "What are the steps to get this done?" is another good question—but be careful here, because your boss may say, "Hey, that's your job—figure it out!" Nevertheless, asking for clarity and direction is important. Even if you just ask about who can help you, your intention is the answer for the messy boss: get clear on the front end, and you minimize the mess on the back end.

Oftentimes, new leaders make a mess because of circumstances beyond their control. There are some steps that I share with my coaching clients, and I want to share them with you, so that you can find some decisiveness inside the uncertainty. Control may be an illusion, but better choices (and better leadership) is always within your grasp.

A lot of new leaders I work with will find themselves wondering how to translate their expertise across generations. For example, consider the story of someone who is promoted internally—maybe because she was the best salesperson—and now she's leading a sales team where some of the folks have twice as much experience as she does!

"Who am I," the new manager wonders, "to tell a 20-year veteran what I need them to do?"

The answer is simple: you are the boss. Not the queen, not the king, but the boss.

> "When you were made a leader, you weren't given a crown, you were given the responsibility to bring out the best in others."
>
> — JACK WELCH, FORMER CHAIRMAN OF GE

Imposter syndrome is a part of all of us. To be specific, that part is trying to protect us from getting out over our skis, from going too far, from making a mistake. What happens, that fearful part whispers, *if people don't like you? You are not qualified for this role!*

As always, the antidote for this destructive part is a dosage of truth serum, on the path to understanding.

The truth is: people don't need to like you in order to do their jobs. The truth is: you are there to bring out the best in others. Not to make friends. Being effective is not the same as being well-liked. Trying to please people is not the same as bringing out the best in them. The truth is: you have the role. Are you qualified to do the role? The answer lies in action. Not contemplation.

What action would someone who was qualified (not an imposter like your part thinks you are) take? What would that effective leader do, or say, or share? Here's the coaching, if you are open to it: Try that. Step into the person that they hired you to be, and step away from the whispers inside your mind that tell you that your career is a fluke, your title is a fake, and your ideas are worthless.

I've been there, and if you are there now, I hope you can hear this: *where you are is not who you are.* Your state of mind can shift with a thought. Whispers from your parts are not a whole solution to anything.

If you are such a people pleaser that you need people to always like you, then guess what? Your parts will win, and the organization will lose. You aren't seeing the whole picture.

When you are asked to lead a team, the organization is counting on you to do what's needed. Just because someone is more of an expert than you are doesn't mean you can't ask them to do something, or to exercise their expertise, or to share that expertise with you. The antidote to intimidation is communication.

Think back to rule #2: What needs to be done?

Not "what needs to be done so your parts can feel a little less insecure," but what needs to be done to help the organization?

Remind yourself who you are—and get back to identifying with yourself—with these quick questions:

- Do you have the ability to recognize expertise and leverage it?
- Do you have to be the smartest person in the room in order to lead the people in the room?
- Do you know what needs to be done?
- Did this organization hire/promote you for a reason?
- For entrepreneurs, did your investors fund you for a reason?
- What are you (or your parts) forgetting, right now?

- What are you (or your parts) making up, right now?
- What's stopping you from asking people to do their jobs? Because, if you're the group leader, isn't that (wait for it) your job?

The imposter part of you wants to find fault, and uses fear to keep you inside of a mess. Lost and alone in a world you do not own, a part of you wants you to believe you are not capable. Let's reach for the truth serum once again:

A. Do you have the skills you need to do this job?
B. Are you able to ask people to do things for you, in a way that's not bossy, controlling, or anything other than helping people to do their job?
C. Can you access coaching and new tools, so that you can feel more confident and confront your parts with greater ease and clarity?
D. ALL OF THE ABOVE

The answer is D. Yes, to all of the above. Yes, you can do this. And, if you can't, it's still a yes. Yes, you can get help. You can get training. You don't have to wait nine years to understand leadership. You've got the answer in your hands.

If the details are elusive, slow down. Ask your team: what am I missing? What do you need from me? Just make sure you set the stage for that question—you are the leader, not Santa Claus. You're not going to turn into a Genie and grant wishes. You are focused on a specific context: namely, how do we communicate so that your parts don't get in the way of you hearing me, as your leader?

Leaders come in all shapes and sizes. How experienced do you have to be in order to be a leader? What's the right age, or education, for a leader? These are the wrong questions, and that's why organizations are making a mess. You are always in charge of your own actions and your own parts. You don't have to live inside of chaos.

The key to leadership is having a vision, and the ability to share it. When it comes down to leadership, whoever tells the best story wins. The ability to communicate clearly—and listen without interference— is crucial to your leadership journey.

Want to avoid being a messy leader? Start listening. Start observing what people need and seeing what needs to be done. If there's something you don't know, go talk to the person who does. Get out of your own way by acknowledging that part of yourself that says you're an imposter.

Everyone experiences imposter syndrome from time to time—that doesn't make it true, or real. It's just a part of you. Look at it this way: Imposter syndrome is just an annoying train of thought. It's not your train. That train of thought won't get you to a useful destination.

The antidote to imposter syndrome is acknowledging your parts. Acknowledge that you are going to feel uncomfortable, especially when you are new to the role. Acknowledge that you can feel like an imposter at any stage in your career!

"You aren't qualified" is a feeling. A feeling that's fleeting, if you stop and just acknowledge that part of yourself. When we come to terms with the part that's trying to protect us—protect us from reaching beyond our grasp—we can actually reach new heights. Because we are calm and neutral when we bring our whole selves into the situation. We are not overthinking things, and answers become clearer.

After all, how do you know that you're not qualified? Here, take this truth serum. (As a coach, I have an unlimited supply.)

Dave, one of my clients, said to me, "I don't know how to hold my team accountable. I don't know how to be a leader for them!" He was really upset. "I want to be empathetic. I want to feel for them. But I also need them to produce!"

Dave was frustrated. Can you relate?

He had worked his way up from being a mechanic to being a maintenance manager. He was running a department of around 20 people, responsible for a pipeline terminal plant just outside of Edmonton. But just before he became a leader, there was a big explosion at the plant. Luckily, no one was hurt. But the safety disaster put everyone on high alert. Because people could have died. What if this failure happens again?

Dave took charge at a time when safety concerns were rampant. Inside a union environment, there was a lot of bureaucracy and standards that needed to be met. And, in Canada, if an employee decides that a work environment is unsafe, they have the ability to refuse work. So if you are asked to work on a gas pipeline, but you think it's leaking natural gas and it's presenting a super-hazard and explosion risk, what are you gonna do? You're going to walk away. You're going to refuse work.

Better to have lost revenues than loss of life. But organizations (and the people who work for them) want safety, and performance—so that they can serve customers.

Dave was a classic Western Canada hockey dad. Heavy-set, super into the Edmonton Oilers, loving family man, salt-of-the-earth kind of guy. A guy who people want to work with, because he loves people.

Empathy is one of his strong suits. Dave wanted a great relationship with his employees (who doesn't?), but what he really needed was for them to produce. In our coaching work, we discovered that those two things (great relationships and great results) are not mutually exclusive. You can have a great relationship (meaning, a relationship based on mutual respect and honesty) where work gets done and people feel good about it. But within that context, Dave was the boss. That meant that he was responsible for both his people and their performance. We weren't going to work on relationships without performance, and vice versa, because the two had to go together. In order to do that, our conversation went back to Dave himself.

Coaching, in large part, is a reframe. At its best, and most transformational, coaching offers a new perspective on an unresolved situation. Could Dave reframe what a "great relationship" looked like? He could, if he brought his parts into the whole.

We worked together to reframe his point of view on himself and his team. Because, like seeing an elephant from a different perspective, changing your point of view changes everything. Facing the elephant's trunk is different from peering into its derriere. Kinda changes what you can do, and what you need to watch out for.

You with me?

Whether you are looking at a situation from the front, the sides, or the back can make a huge impact. That's true when dealing with teams as well. And when considering how your parts come together to make you whole.

At the end of our second session, Dave said to me, "You made me believe that I'm a real leader." That objective—Dave as leader—became the elephant in the room. So naturally, I wanted to talk about it.

Was that "real leader" a matter of belief… or understanding?

I saw him for who he really was. I saw beyond who his parts told him he was.

There are things that go beyond belief. Those things are just… true. Like sand on the beach, or birds in the air. He was, and is, a real leader. He just couldn't see it.

Did I mention that truth serum isn't really a drug, it's more or less an observation? Because when we see what is true, we literally go beyond belief.

You may not believe in gravity. In fact, you don't have to. You don't have to believe that when I drop this egg on the floor, it will break. Because it will. That's just how eggs work. If you don't believe me, it doesn't matter. Notice that your lack of belief just made a mess. Hmmm, maybe that egg test wasn't such a good idea? But I digress.

When we move into the realm of physics (how things work), belief takes a back seat. I was thrilled that I helped Dave to believe in himself. But it really was a matter of physics. And then, some engineering.

See, I studied engineering at MIT. And, when you get right down to it, I approach life, and leadership, like an engineer. I consider the tools that are available, and I work with what is to build what could be.

And with Dave, what was right in front of me was a leader. Did I need to bang two sticks together, like Tony Robbins, and play loud music to help awaken the giant within? No.

Nothing against Tony Robbins, he's helped a lot of people, but let's get real. Not rah-rah. My coaching is not motivational, it's factual. If you see things in a new way, you will do things in a new way. And you will find a path to self-leadership, going beyond your parts to seeing the whole.

We talked about how Dave could introduce a new level of accountability in his one-on-one meetings, setting new standards and receiving positive feedback along the way. Physics, and engineering. We were talking about doing the doable (which is often the antidote to overcoming the impossible).

Having conversations? That's doable. So that's what Dave did. He took the tools that he had (his wits and the ability to talk to his team) and he went to work. He talked about the importance of standards, and he let people know where they stood. And he let them know what he needed. Turns out, he got more than what he expected.

Dave was pleasantly surprised, to say the least, but it was no surprise to me. His people responded really well.

Human beings like to know that they are doing good work. Feedback helps us to navigate the chaos! We like to know that we are being measured, and that there is a standard or benchmark that guides our progress. Sometimes, just letting people know that you are paying attention is a way to step up as a leader. What's the power of acknowledgment—really noticing someone—in your organization? Are you catching people doing things right, offering encouragement along the way? Or are you silent until a problem turns into a mess, showing up to scold people and slap them on the wrist?

Discouragement as a leadership strategy: How's that working out for you?

Often, it's clear feedback that's missing on teams with a messy boss: you don't really know how well you are doing. You don't know that there's a mess until you are in the middle of it. And then, punishment and bad reviews rain down on everyone—which is more chaotic than necessary. But for Dave's group, mistakes meant safety issues. Lost time. Lost wages. Maybe even, in a worst-case scenario, loss of life. Dave needed people to know that he was watching.

You know why?

So that he could ask them to watch out, too.

If you want to engineer greater success for your team, get clear on the goals. Catch people doing something right. Notice what is working, before there's a mess. And when there's a "clean up on aisle seven" because somebody made a mess, don't look the other way. Stay in the conversation. Pick up a mop, or whatever tools are nearby. Do what you can to help with the clean-up.

Don't scold. Be bold. Be bold in your encouragement of the behavior you want to see. That doesn't mean ignoring what's wrong, or missing. But instead of *finding* fault, try *reminding* instead.

Remind people who they are, and what they are capable of. Remind people that everyone makes mistakes, and everyone has the ability to look at things in a new way.

And if you're getting some resistance to that last statement, maybe it's time to hire a coach! Applying pressure and scolding adults is not a strategy for success.

Nobody works well with a gun to their head. Being the boss who puts pressure on people is a way to encourage mediocrity. Set standards, guide people towards the results you want, and recognize the power of encouragement. Remind people of what they can do—and let them know that you need them to do it! You need their whole selves, at work—not just a part, but the whole.

If your team is not performing, look at how much discouragement and pressure you have in your organization. If you see a culture of encouragement, but people aren't performing, look at your communication. What's the conversation you need to have, but won't? Are you chasing after higher employee engagement scores, and sacrificing quality and customer satisfaction along the way? Is everyone smiling, but your plant is an absolute safety hazard and a simmering disaster waiting to happen? Those smiles won't last. And your shareholders will frown.

Again, what needs to be done?

Everyone wants happy employees. But if people are not held accountable, so that they can be productive, no one is going to be happy. Including your customers, your boss, and, quite frankly, your team members. That's right.

The people-pleaser boss is a messy leader. People-pleasing is a recipe for confusion because goals become unclear. Accountability doesn't matter as much as being pals with everybody on the team. Dave's role in the energy company was part of the oil and gas *business,* not oil and gas *friends*. Remember your purpose, as the leader—and help your team to do the same. The mission is what matters. Without a clear mission, you're going to have a mess.

Get clear on your ability to share what needs to be said, and be willing to hear it when feedback comes back around. One of the things that I liked best about my former bosss, Susan, is her ability to give meaningful feedback. When I asked her, "What can I do better?" she always had ideas for continuous improvement. She knows me, and I know she only wants me to be better, because we shared the same agenda. We're both former athletes, and we focus on our performance without hesitation or personal interference. In other words, we communicate effectively without taking things personally.

For Susan and me, we don't let personal sensitivities get in the way of personal productivity. That's not easy in this day and age, when people can be easily triggered. Notice that I said "people"—so that means you and that means me! But I've learned that making the impersonal personal is how a messy situation gets started. My parts want to protect me, but they end up making a mess of things, over-indexing on fear and control when what I really need to do is listen and speak from the heart.

What my coaching helps teams and organizations to realize is that effective communication is based on mutual respect, inside an understanding of triggers and sensitivities (caused by our parts). But ultimately, there is a shared commitment around mutually identified goals that brings us back to ourselves. That shared agreement is what allows us to approach work impersonally. That way, our parts are calmly participating in a way that's useful, not obstructive.

For Dave, the standards he rolled out in private meetings are now part of their team standards. His monthly team meetings have an accountability component, where everyone sees the progress of the team. Comparisons are used to help influence people to meet a standard, and a healthy competition encourages people to exceed it. In fact, if someone is under-performing, they aren't shamed and put into the penalty box. Others step up and help to find ways to make sure that everyone keeps the standards and safety in place.

When someone comes to me and says, "I don't know how to hold people accountable," that statement is either true or false, right?

For Dave, he said he didn't *know how to* hold people accountable. I wasn't going to call him a liar, but I wanted to explore that statement further. Was that really true—that he didn't know how to hold people accountable? I asked him some questions about other management situations, and we discovered something. He actually did know how to hold people accountable.

So, knowledge wasn't the problem. Skills and talents were in place. There was not a skill gap or an information gap.

Execution was missing. And I wondered why.

The reframe was around the importance of accountability in our work together. When he saw that accountability actually allowed him to be a real leader, he became more of himself (not less). For his employees, he was now *more than* their friend. Because being *more than* a friend means keeping your team safe, helping them perform better, and helping them to be better than they would be if you weren't there to lead them. Dave was helping people to be empowered, and informed, about what needed to be done. And creating an atmosphere of clear communication, so that mutual responsibility was becoming part of the company culture.

"I don't know how to…" takes a new shape when you reframe it to, "Now I really want to…" Because when you want to do something, the "how to" follows. Your engineering brain kicks in, even if you're not an engineer, and you start solving problems and finding resources. That is, when you really *want* to. If that's not the case, and you really do have a "how-to" problem, it's really a *want-to* problem.

If you really *want to* solve it, you'll enroll in a class, watch a YouTube video, read a book, or hire a coach.

Desire drives results. As crazy as it sounds, if you fall in love with a problem, you will find a new way to solve it.

That culture changed with Dave. One guy. One hockey fan who decided to go beyond belief—and step into who he was.

Some organizations remind me that leaders can make a mess. Dave reminds me that a real leader can make a difference.

BREAKDOWN TO BREAK THROUGH

1. Messy bosses often make decisions too quickly, which can result in missed details and poorly communicated instructions. To manage this, take a step back and slow down the process. Ensure that all instructions and expectations are clearly communicated and thoroughly understood before moving forward.
2. Prioritize the most critical aspects of a project to avoid getting bogged down by less important details. By identifying and focusing on the key objectives, you can streamline the process and ensure that essential tasks are completed efficiently.
3. Delegate at the appropriate level for the task and the person who's assigned to the task. How you delegate should vary from someone who's an expert to someone who's never done the task before.
4. When working with a messy boss, actively seek clarification and feedback to ensure that you understand expectations and deliverables.

Regular check-ins can help address any misunderstandings and prevent issues from escalating.

EXPLORATIONS

1. Reflect on a time when a project or task went awry due to hurried or unclear instructions. What specific details were missing or misunderstood, and how did this affect the outcome? Have you ever experienced a messy situation, as defined in this chapter, that wasn't based on a communication issue?
2. What questions can you think of that would help create clarity in your next interaction with your own team and your own employees?
3. How does your leadership team encourage dialogue to create clarity?
4. What practices do you employ, as a leader, to avoid becoming a messy boss? How do you vary your delegation based on your team's expertise, task complexity, and criticality?

CHAPTER 10

THE CHAOS OF THE GHOST MANAGER

> "You can't be afraid of offending people. You can't try and go down the middle of the road. You have to take a stand on something."
>
> — PHIL KNIGHT, FOUNDER OF NIKE

> "The very essence of leadership is that you have to have vision. You can't blow an uncertain trumpet."
>
> — THEODORE HESBURGH, PRESIDENT EMERITUS OF THE UNIVERSITY OF NOTRE DAME

Do you believe in ghosts?

If you see one in the workplace, you'll never forget it.

I'm not talking about an ancient haunted spirit coming back to torment those who would dare to use the copy machine. Not the poltergeists that bedevil your Microsoft Teams login, or the evil gremlins that live inside your point of sale system.

I'm talking about the ghost manager.

"Ghost manager" is the leadership style of the cowardly boss. If you have one, it's pretty scary. If you are one, your employees are feeling haunted by an eerie and often unseen presence.

How do you know if you are working for a ghost manager?
Here are some key characteristics:

1. When you need something, they vanish.
2. They take the easy way out and disappear when you ask for support.
3. They act like they don't know what they actually know—especially if it helps to avoid risk, visibility, or confrontation.
4. They ignore what's dragging everyone down (see #2).
5. They are constantly blaming others.
6. They are so overloaded with "busyness" that they lose sight of the business—unable to notice what's really going on, and what really needs to be done.
7. Ghost managers make you feel like you are on an island. You feel unsupported because you can't get answers, feedback or engagement when you need it most.

HOW TO AVOID BEING HAUNTED

In my experience, calling someone a coward is risky business. Sort of like calling someone a liar. Seems like a good way to start a fight—or at the very least, make someone very defensive. Circumstances can make cowards of us all—that part exists in even the bravest and strongest among us. But calling anyone a "coward" isn't helping anybody to heal, improve or (to put it bluntly) stop being an asshole. Let's look at the antidote instead.

Lots of things can turn us towards fear. You may already be thinking that fear is at the root of all of these chaotic and negative behaviors. You're right. For some, the basic fear (of not meeting goals, of not being the best, or whatever the case may be) can lead people to lash out, yelling, cursing, and (yes) even resorting to violence. For others, that same root impulse—that same fear—doesn't lead to any action at all. In fact, in this case, fear leads to retreat. Withdrawal. Complete and utter inaction.

Fear drives the behavior of the passive-aggressive boss, the abusive narcissist, and yes, the cowardly boss. All of these types—these parts, if you will—are victims of fear. Just as we all are, from time to time.

Being effective means not letting an isolated incident turn into a pattern of behavior, where our parts control the pattern of response. Breaking a pattern is always the first step in moving from chaos to clarity when it comes to dealing with fear.

Unlike the other types, where our parts drive a particular action or series of actions, the ghost manager is characterized by inaction. Deflection. A lack of responsibility. In some regards, the cowardly boss is similar to the messy boss—leaving things undone, unable to confront (or even converse) with team members, avoiding decisions and more. But there's a key difference.

A messy boss won't give clear direction and deadlines; their communication is murky and incomplete. The ghost manager—another way of saying "cowardly boss"—just ghosts you. Their response to the game of business is to choose not to play. Their favorite response is being unresponsive.

When you go to a ghost manager and say something like, "Hey, here's a problem and we need to fix this," they will deflect. Or if they do address the problem, it's gonna be someone else's problem. Someone else's decision. Someone else's fault.

A ghost manager engages in blamestorming. Instead of offering ideas and innovation, they find ways to blame others. Anything to avoid making a decision, having a conversation, or (dare I say it?) doing their job.

The ghost manager offers the worst possible interpretation of a classic Steve Jobs quote. Jobs, the guru of Apple who gave us the modern Mac, the iPhone, iPad, and iTunes (the precursor to Apple Music), famously said, "It doesn't make sense to hire smart people and then tell them what to do. We hire smart people so they can tell us what to do."

So, when you have something you need from a ghost manager, this cowardly person will tell you, "That's why I hired you. You figure it out."

This kind of misdirection and lack of support happens all the time. But let's face the facts: we don't think of ourselves as cowards, right? But let me ask you: have you ever experienced a sense of overwhelm? A place where the chaos and uncertainty feel so great that you just shut down, lock up, and can't seem to do anything? That's how this part shows up on an individual basis—and we've all been there.

Notice, however, that overwhelm is a state of mind. It's different from overload, which is when a circuit receives too much power, or a machine is asked to bear more weight than it can, and the system is overloaded. Overwhelm can be as simple as, "Where the hell are my car keys?!" Notice that overload is the state of a system. Overwhelm is a state of mind.

To test this theory, consider the change from "Where are my car keys?"—the sense of frustration and overwhelm that arises after you've been looking under the chair, checking the hoodie you wore yesterday, and feeling around under the bed for 15 minutes. It can be a little overwhelming! Then, what happens when you find your keys?

Boom. All is well.

From chaos to certainty, the journey is exactly one thought. Calmness returns.

However, when a circuit is overloaded, it is blown. There's no change until you replace the system that has failed. Notice that, in the case of overwhelm, you are experiencing chaos—not a system failure. And, inside of overwhelm, the key idea is to keep moving. In the simple scenario of the lost car keys, the best way to go about the search is always: calmly. In a way that keeps your parts from screaming at those around you, or accusing your dog of stealing your car keys. (He didn't. Trust me, I asked him twice).

Notice the difference between overload and overwhelm. We use these words interchangeably, but that's not really accurate. Inaccurate labels can lead to over-indexing and activating a part of ourselves that doesn't need to come into play. Yet, for the ghost manager, that's the game that they are playing.

For the cowardly ghost manager, fear deactivates everything—masquerading as overload, it's just overwhelm. Fear finds itself in the driver's seat, and the ghost manager puts on the brakes. They are not going anywhere. If you work around this chaotic manager, neither are you.

You feel like you are on an island, unsupported and unseen, as your leader refuses to respond. I have a client, a COO at an artificial intelligence (AI) company, and her CEO boss is a hot mess. She tries to meet with him, to discuss vital operational issues, and he keeps canceling meetings. His leadership style is *dis*-engagement. Avoidance. The end result is pure frustration.

As with any kind of unexpected and seemingly counterproductive behavior, a little understanding can help navigate the chaos.

Fear focuses on implications. Our minds race to engineer the outcomes of a particular situation or series of events. Even though we know that no one can predict the future, our parts always try to. "I know how this will end," our parts whisper, "and it's *bad*. Don't do anything! Don't touch it! Don't take responsibility! Don't let them pin this on you!" The misuse of imagination—another way to describe fear and worry —turns us into cowards, and we avoid what needs to be done.

DEFLECTION

A messy boss will sit down with you and create a project plan. They will give you instruction, but it's probably incomplete, half-baked and/or cryptic. It's messy. The ghost manager just won't offer anything. "Is it ok if I do *X*?" you ask the cowardly boss. "Yeah, ok" they say, rubber stamping your request—and making sure you bear all of the responsibility for your choice, with none of their support. You might think you are asking for their backing, but the ghost manager sees your request as a report. In other words, you are telling them what you are going to do.

And if it goes wrong, that's on you.

SPOTLIGHT SYNDROME

Some are afraid of being in the spotlight. Especially when our fearful parts begin seeing spotlights everywhere. Spotlight syndrome is a psychological phenomenon where we start to overestimate how much others are noticing us. Overestimating our own visibility can lead our parts to over-index—making us want to hide, like cowards, when it's really unnecessary. Withdrawal, and social anxiety, can be the result—according to *Psychology Today*. Seems unfair to compare a condition, like social anxiety, with cowardice. But the behavior—pulling back from people and situations—can be similar to over-protection. Are you over-estimating your visibility in social situations, in the project plan, in the eyes of your leadership team? Are you pulling back, as a result?

STAY SAFE OUT THERE

Safety matters. Especially psychological safety. In Amy Edmondsons' groundbreaking book, *The Fearless Organization,* she says that, "Psychological safety is broadly defined as a climate in which people are comfortable expressing and being themselves." Creating an environment where people feel free to speak their minds, share ideas and discover new solutions is the goal—and brave interactions can't happen if people are frozen with fear, unwilling to respond, unable to engage.

We have to create cultures where it is safe to express ideas, ask questions, and admit mistakes. And, for the leaders and managers out there: to do so in an environment of engagement and support. That engagement requires dialogue: clarifying goals, establishing account-ability and, if necessary, delivering consequences. "Psychological safety," Edmonson writes, "is about candor, about making it possible for productive disagreement and free exchange of ideas." If you ghost your employee, or your team, you disengage. No exchange can take place, and therefore, no progress. Helping companies to create a culture where psychological safety is woven into the fabric of the organization is one of my greatest strengths. And, in my work, engaging one-on-one with cowardly bosses can be a compassionate way to create change from the inside out. Because we create a dialogue with the parts, inside a safe space, so that candor (truth) can help bring order to internal chaos.

Safety matters. But if you are always taking the safe route, you may be a cowardly boss. Someone close to me, a brilliant and well-educated guy, one of the smartest people I know, spent his entire career in a government job—basically, punching below his weight so he could take the easy way out and collect a pension. That's not to say that government jobs are easy, or that there's anything wrong with that choice. However, as someone who has built his career around helping people reach their potential, it made me sad to consider what might have been for this guy. I felt sorry for someone who didn't want to try for something more. True, it's his career and his choice. It's like going to the vast buffet of life, where you can have delicious food from all over the world, and you choose stale crackers and a carrot stick. There's more on offer, if you just look around!

Have you ever seen someone who looks like they are retired at their desk? An empty suit? Someone who's afraid to ever really try their hardest or put in real effort, for fear that being seen would make them somehow unsafe?

Are they eating a carrot stick?

We all have fears of not being good enough. Seen in a positive light, this impulse could be called "conscientiousness," "thoughtfulness," or "attention to detail." But when those positive impulses take us from trying to do a good job to being afraid to do our jobs, we stop trying. Engagement drops off a cliff. And, for the disengaged and cowardly ghost manager, they send a silent scream to everyone on the team: there's no need to try in this organization. Results don't matter. Trust takes a holiday. And imposter syndrome becomes a plague.

Notice that psychological safety, innovation and new ideas can co-exist—in fact, they help us to navigate chaos! That is, if our fearful parts don't get in the way. Here's how we can cope with the spotlight effect, and calm our parts that might be holding us back:

1. **Challenge Your Beliefs**—A simple question that I ask my coaching clients is, "Is that true?" Any fearful situation is best examined from this perspective. The question comes from the work of Byron Katie, the author of *Loving What Is*. It's the first of four questions she uses to gently but firmly ask people to take a fresh look at a situation or relationship. Where could this question help you to reframe or re-evaluate a particularly scary situation? Is there really a danger, or are you creating a circumstance around a possible outcome? And, if you imagine something is going to happen, how can you really know it's true? The key here is to challenge yourself with compassion. Be kind to yourself as you ask this question—you are not calling yourself a liar! You're just taking a fresh look at something we all do from time to time—misusing our imaginations. We create stuff to scare ourselves, and—like worrying about the monster under your bed when you were six years old—you just have to calmly wonder, Is that true?

2. **Put Your Attention on Others**—When fear grips us at work, it might be because of a self-consciousness we all experience. Psychologists call it an "illusion of transparency," which is a tendency to think that our internal state of mind is visible to others. News flash: your internal state of mind is not seen—it's a mystery to everyone but you. Notice what other people are really seeing, and sensing. Often it's less than what spotlight syndrome might lead you to believe—especially the dialogue that's going on inside your mind. That's according to psychologist Arlin Cunic, the author of *The Anxiety Workbook*. Shifting your focus to others can help you to take your attention off

of yourself. Try moving from self-awareness to situational awareness, and see if you can find some new ways of thinking about your "visibility." Extra credit if the way you think about yourself and the way you are coming across is: "not at all." What shows up for you, if you could embrace this idea—and stop trying to impress?

3. **Try Role Reversal**—When something makes you feel like you are in the spotlight, Cunic says, think about how you would respond if the same thing happened to somebody else. If a friend misspoke, would it be a big deal? If a co-worker made a small mistake during a presentation, would you even think much of it? "Once you realize that other people feel the same way about your own actions, you'll probably start to feel more at ease and less like you are standing in front of a spotlight," Cunic shares.

4. **What Else Could This Mean?**—When my clients begin explaining a situation at work, the story is never just a series of facts and figures. Interpretation comes into the story, as it always does (it's part of our nature). We interpret events, and create an interpretation that leads to fear—even cowardice—because we are certain that we know the implications of a particular circumstance. Using the question above, "Is that true?" we have to recognize that what is true is not a matter of faith or belief, it's just true. Like water boiling at 100 degrees centigrade, or the law of gravity. You don't need to believe in the ability of water to boil in order for it to happen, because (checks the stove, sees water boiling) it's just true. And, when I find my clients interpreting circumstances in ways that make me curious, I start to wonder: what else could this mean? Coaching, for me, is about offering a safe space for sharing, where I listen with intense curiosity (not judgment). My coaching often helps people to see a kinder interpretation of events—offering some compassion instead of catastrophe,

if people are willing to look in that direction. Are you? Are you able to step back, and ask yourself, "What else could this mean?" Because a different interpretation of events might calm your parts, and lead you away from fear, as you discover a new course of action. Taking a fresh look requires what Patrick Lencioni calls interpersonal courage. "It's something that is really lacking in most organizations," says the best-selling author of *Five Dysfunctions of a Team* and *Death by Meeting*. "People who work for these companies suffer when people can't speak to one another in truth."

Ultimately if you work for a cowardly boss, there are several steps inside the antidote that you need to consider.

1. **Have the Conversation**—if you're thinking about the conversation you need to have with Tallia, a person whose name I just made up, here's the deal: you're right. Trust your instincts. Have the conversation. She's been avoiding you? You've been avoiding her? Consider that the conversation is never going to be tougher than it is in your mind. Maybe it's time to send a message with a simple subject: "Can we find a time to talk about *X*?" (Or is it a text? WhatsApp? Whatever.) Just don't say, "We need to talk," or use that as a subject line. This kind of directness can be seen as confrontation and can create anxiety from the other person (who's already struggling with some challenges around fear). Don't create further stress—especially if the thing you need to discuss isn't stressful at all. Better to come at the conversation as a "Meeting Request," or perhaps, "Time to talk?"—and offer an idea of what you'd like to discuss.

   Offer times during the day today. Connect with Tallia. Connect with her—and if you don't know the difference between connection and confrontation, maybe *we* should talk. If you work in the same office, go see her. Don't let things fester. Like the garbage sitting out on your front porch, it's not going to smell any better tomorrow. Take out the metaphorical trash, and clear the air. Is Tallia a cowardly boss, a ghost manager? Stop slinging labels and start finding solutions. Patrick Lencioni says, in *The Five Dysfunctions of a Team*, "if you don't have conflict around ideas or circumstances or situation, it ferments into conflict around people." Conversation is the antidote to conflict, despite what your parts may be telling you. Consider how you can break a pattern, and say what needs to be said.

3. **Speed Matters:** Look at the narratives that you are creating in your own head, right now, courtesy of your overactive parts. These stories are keeping you stuck, keeping you from action, keeping you from the conversation that just might cure the situation. Letting ideas fester and ferment, as Lencioni says, can turn you into a coward. Overwhelm looks like overload, in this scenario. What if you didn't have to script out everything you were going to say, including writing the dialogue for whoever your Tallia might be? Perhaps an intention is what's needed, and an impulse for action. If you think you can't have a spontaneous conversation, ask yourself a quick question: "Is that true?" I've had times where I've been dreading a necessary conversation, but instead of planning every nuance and every move, I do something much more important: I take the first step. I do the thing that is the opposite of the cowardly boss: I engage. Starting a conversation is like turning on a light switch: the darkness is defeated, and you can see things more clearly. But understanding how to have a difficult conversation is also part of the antidote for the cowardly boss.

4. **Start at the Very Beginning:** what would happen if you began by stating your feelings? I'm not suggesting you confess your sins (or theirs). But some simple language around your experience of recent events is something that is true—because it

is your experience. You are not blaming someone (that's the move of the cowardly boss). You are expressing your reaction to events. You own your feelings, and you speak up to find clarity. In this regard, your story is not only inarguable, it opens up a deeper understanding for the person right in front of you. Phrases like, "I was frustrated when…" or, "When you kept canceling the meeting, I felt…"

Perhaps you are an engineer, like me, and you think that feelings are no substitute for facts. But no matter what your education or job description, you are a human being. And the fact is: we all have feelings. Feelings of confusion. Feelings that there's something we need to discuss. Feeling like there's something between us, or something that would make your work life easier.

Start there. "Here's what I felt, here's what I saw/heard/experienced," and then: "here's what I think the problem was."

5. **Candor and Importance:** recognize the value in candor (being honest) and you will bring the ghost back to life. Can you candidly and frankly tell the person in front of you that they matter to you? Let me be clear: I'm not suggesting that you showcase your desire to please, or to try and flatter someone in an effort to get a result. That's manipulation, not frankness. Be honest. Don't kiss somebody's ass and call it a conversation. Candor means telling the truth. Imagine the Vice President of Sales and Marketing sitting down with the lead scientist in the research lab. She says, "Your input matters to me, and without guidance from R&D, the sales team is going to end up over-promising on the new products. That's why I need your help." Notice that asking for help is not a declaration of weakness. Support is the key to any exchange, born out of mutual respect, where compassionate candor leads the way. The fact of the matter, and it is True with a capital T, is that we need each other. Withholding information, for whatever reason,

can result in a lie of omission. When someone is a manager or a leader and they don't engage, they leave others as less than what they could be. Less than what they are. Let people know that they mean something to you—not in an attempt to curry favor, but in a clear and direct way that candidly expresses the feeling behind the conversation. Let people know that they matter! After all, that's why this conversation—whatever it may be—is important. Don't let cowardice win. A frank conversation is the antidote.

6. **What If the Ghost Won't Show Up?**—Always have a mentor. Always. If you really want to get serious about your career, and your results, get a coach. But a good coach will tell you: internal resources are the key to external results. When I was working in heavy industry, my boss was a ghost manager. He had certain things he cared about, which covered half of the job. And then, there were things he didn't care about—that was the other half of the job. So, if he didn't care about some aspect of the work at hand—but you needed him to give you a hand -he'd just say, "Go ask somebody else." Meanwhile, if the topic was something he cared about, you could get trapped in his office as he talked over, around and through a subject that was of deep interest. I ended up making friends with a co-worker named Jim, somebody who knew where everything was: internal resources, skeletons in the closet, etc. You name it he knew it. "Jim," I would say, "who do I need to talk to about this? What do I need to know about this situation or this department or whatever?" He would point me in the right direction. When you have a good mentor, and good internal resources, you don't have to be afraid of ghosts.

Remember the Seinfeld episode, where George sleeps under his desk? George stays up all night, watching *The Omen Trilogy*. So, over breakfast, he tells Jerry how tired he is. "Can't you take a nap at work?"

Jerry asks. George can't because his office has a wall of windows—everyone would see him sleeping. "Ah, I love a good nap," George says. "It's the only thing that gets me out of bed in the morning."

George ends up hiring a contractor to build out this elaborate system of shelves and blankets, under his desk, so he can get some rest.

Is your cowardly boss hiding under the desk? Are you?

Are you hiding on zoom meetings, with your camera off, because it feels a little too much like a spotlight is on you? Consider that if people don't know what you are doing, and how you are contributing, don't be surprised if you are overlooked for a promotion or a new opportunity. You might be creating chaos, not capitalizing on it.

Whatever your situation: it's okay to be afraid.

That's right. I said it. We all have fears. Huge rugby players can be afraid of spiders. Tiny grandmas can be fearless. Fear isn't a function of size, age or gender. It's a state of mind. Worrying about things is part of being human. Understanding how fear works is part of being effective.

Next time a part of you jumps into action, triggering a fear response, take a moment to pause. What is your part trying to tell you? Inside our parts are good intentions, just poor execution. A misuse of imagination causes us to worry. To stop making progress. To withdraw. To climb under our desks.

Don't. It doesn't have to be like this. Even if you have a pattern of behavior, a history of a particular response, remember: you are not driven purely by instinct. Notice that there's a part of you that's afraid.

That doesn't make you a coward. It makes you a human being.

Fear is a part of the human experience. We have all been there. All of us.

Parts can be messengers, when we stop to really observe what's going on. Notice what the part of you is asking you to do.

1. Is this a supportive behavior, or not? Is this an old habit, or a new idea?
2. Would you be open to a new idea?

3. Would that part of you be open to a different set of actions, and a different response?

4. How about just exploring a new pathway, like a science experiment—would that work?

As you re-interpret events, ask your part, "What else could this mean?" or perhaps this variation: "What else could this be?"

A client came to me, on the verge of applying for a new position, and she was filled with fear. In her situation, her fear was creating even more chaos inside her mind. In our conversation, we leaned in on something different. Seeking clarity amidst the chaos, we leaned in on love.

We talked about finding love and compassion for the part of her that was trying to protect her. Could she learn to love the part of her that was trying to shield her and shepherd her towards a new career? "In order for us to get somewhere new," I said, sharing something that just seemed very true to me, "we have to do new things. If you are going to visit a town you've never seen before, you're going to encounter some strange roads. Is that cause for alarm, or what we should expect?"

There's no concern, only new scenery to observe. What if she observed her fear, recognizing that it was a part of her—but not the whole picture? What if, I wondered out loud, she saw that she had to make decisions that would lead her to a new destination? Those decisions involved making peace with the part of her that was trying to warn her of danger up ahead. There was no danger—only new roads.

Loving your parts is easy when you see that your parts are you. Does that make sense? It's like my left thumb. It's a part of my hand. But that part is me. Just like my shoulders and my elbows—they are parts of the whole.

There can be power in a little bit of movement, a little conversation, a small step leading to big results. A conversation with a part can help to make you whole —and the next chapter will show you how. Meanwhile, don't let fear stop you from taking the first step. Nothing more, nothing less. Just the first step. The reminders at the end of the chapter will help point you in the right direction.

Fear is always with us. We don't need to fight fear. We don't need to "feel the fear and do it anyway." Before we do anything, and in order to get going, we need to embrace fear as a part of ourselves. And then, we need to find another response, another path, another way of seeing things. Those options are critical. Because the difference between the ghost manager and a highly effective leader is what they do when that fear shows up.

PS: you don't have to be afraid of ghosts.

BREAKDOWN TO BREAK THROUGH

1. **Foster Psychological Safety**: Encourage an environment where everyone feels comfortable sharing ideas, asking questions, and admitting mistakes. Without psychological safety, progress stalls, and disengagement rises.

2. **Challenge and Reframe**: Regularly challenge your own and others' beliefs about fear and risk. Use questions like "Is that true?" to reframe potentially paralyzing fears and encourage a more balanced perspective on challenges. Remember to use constructive curiosity, not confrontation, in your inquiry

3. **Engage Directly**: Refrain from avoiding difficult conversations. Instead, approach them with intention, curiosity and clarity. Frame discussions as opportunities for connection and problem-solving rather than conflict.

4. **Cultivate Candor and Accountability**: Promote honesty and openness. Address issues directly, recognize the value of clear communication, and encourage others to do the same to prevent issues from festering.

EXPLORATIONS

1. Have you ever found yourself avoiding a conversation or decision due to fear? What helped you overcome that fear, or what might have helped you in hindsight?
2. Think about a time when you just didn't show up. You walked away. You didn't play. What created the ghost in you? Was that the right decision? What would you do differently, and what did you take away from your previous choice?
3. What does safety mean to you, and to your organization? How do you think a lack of psychological safety impacts team performance? Is psychological safety a state of mind, or a set of boundaries, requirements and protocols that ensure safety exists? Who or what is responsible for psychological safety in your organization? Where does safety come from—in the literal, and in the abstract ("feeling safe")?
4. How do you foster a psychologically safe environment for yourself and your team? What behaviors can you practice to encourage psychological safety? What behaviors do you need to change in yourself or your team that discourage psychological safety?

CHAPTER 11

THE CLARITY OF CONNECTING TO SELF

> *"You are the sky, everything else is just weather."*
>
> — *PEMA CHÖDRÖN, AMERICAN NUN, BUDDHIST TEACHER, AND AUTHOR*
>
> ---
>
> *"Self is the sky, your parts are just the weather."*
>
> — *SUNNY STRASBURG LMFT, WORLD-RENOWNED LICENSED PSYCHEDELIC TRAUMA THERAPIST AND AUTHOR OF* THE THERADELIC APPROACH

How often do you play?

I'm not talking about *Candy Crush*. I'm talking about really engaging with the feeling of *calm playfulness*—the kind of feeling you had when you were a kid. Like on the playground. Do you remember?

Most of us forget. I know I do, from time to time. But when I show up at my best—and when my clients do the same—life doesn't feel like work. And work feels like play.

There's a feeling that we discover. We don't have to reach for it or search aimlessly for it or develop enough grit to earn it. The feeling is waiting for us. Always. Like the floor underneath a carpet—it's there, even if we can't see it.

Turning work into play: what would that be like for you?

It sounds outrageous. Impossible. You may be thinking, "Rob, you don't understand the stress and the pressure and the responsibility and the assholes I have to work with… the chaos in my office is crazy! Have you lost your mind?"

No, my friend. I've found it. If you're open to it, I'd like to help you to do the same.

I'm not saying that you need to bring dolls, frisbees and toys to the office, or pretend you are Iron Man before you go into your next meeting. True, those behaviors are pretty playful. But there's a practical playfulness that doesn't require you to act like a child. Practical playfulness is where you simply remember who you are, underneath all of the layers of life and experience—the things that have influenced and fed and strengthened your parts. But what's underneath those parts that keep on trying to run the show?

Practical playfulness is like pulling up that old carpet and discovering a beautiful hardwood floor underneath. Notice how the whole room looks different?

Away from our screens, Xboxes and headsets, there's a different kind of game available. I'm talking about the game of life—and how you show up for the people that matter most to you.

Like any game, you're probably wondering about the objective. And the rules. What happens if you win?

Well, for this game, victory means nothing less than finding out who you really are. Discovering what you really want. Finding new ways of showing up in the world. Because the way you show up is what creates the world around you.

Have you ever had a stressful or challenging situation that suddenly felt very different—even though nothing had changed? It's possible to be surrounded by chaos, and not feel stress, isn't it? It's possible to be kind and compassionate to yourself, even if maybe that's not how you were raised. You don't have to play a game where you treat yourself like shit and expect that kind of self-talk to help you improve your performance. Or your mood. Or anything, really. Change is always a possibility. You can give to yourself, and to others, a kind of compassion that perhaps you weren't given… or you haven't been willing to give to yourself.

Because (and this news is just in): you are not a piece of shit. Despite what your parts might be trying to tell you. Despite what your boyfriend said, or you momma used to say, or whatever. Contrary to popular belief, discouragement does not lead to peak performance. Maybe iron sharpens iron, but hitting yourself in the head with a hammer is not gonna sharpen anybody.

Believe me. I know.

I had a part of me that thought that suicide was the answer.

That's right. Suicide.

A part of me was saying, "Suicide will protect you."

The thought wasn't just showing up in the middle of a really rough Thursday afternoon. I woke up, and the thought was there. Like a nagging pain in my back, it never went away. And certain moves would really *really* remind me of the pain. My part would come to the rescue: "Your death will make all of this go away."

I recognize that may not make sense. Death looked like a relief? But that's what it was.

I had thoughts that the best way forward was to end it all. I tried going through CBT, or cognitive behavioral therapy. The end result was that I ended up inside a logic argument with myself.

"Logically," the voice inside my head would say, "if you want this pain to go away, you should kill yourself."

Rationalizing, in the spirit of CBT, I would argue with this voice: "You are wrong, and let me tell you why…" Yet the reasons I came up with seemed to fall short, and the pain wasn't going away. "If you want the pain to go away," my hyper-logical voice would say, digging in even deeper and trying hard to win, "you need to end it all." The scary part? Logically, it made sense! But somehow, somewhere deep down, I wanted something different.

I wanted to live.

I just didn't know how.

Instead of arguing inside my head, based on my therapeutic journey into my past, I pivoted. Instead of confrontation around logic, I discovered compassion around my parts. I discovered a new possibility. And IFS (Internal Family Systems) literally saved my life.

"I understand, in this moment, that suicide feels like the only answer," I was able to say to my protector part, under guided therapy. "Ending it all looks like it will end the pain, right? I understand where you are coming from." I said this to the part of me that was stuck inside a loop of self-annihilation.

"And I love you."

That's right. I embraced the killer in me.

"I love you because you're trying to help me." From inside an embrace, I asked the part, "What else could this mean?" I was reflecting on the circumstances of my life that seemed to lead my part to reach only one conclusion, over and over again.

"What else could this be? Can you help me to find a new solution, another possibility?" I asked, looking for a new direction. I was speaking to a part of me, and to all of me. To my higher self, and my lower impulses, all at the same time. For me, segmenting the parts—under the IFS framework—literally made me whole. And brought me back to life.

The irony is that facing the seriousness of suicide helped me to find a new way to play. We don't get to choose our thoughts, but we can always choose how we react to them. A more lighthearted approach to the game of life is one that can help you to win—but only 100% of the time.

Epictetus, the ancient Greek philosopher, said it best: "It's not what happens to you, but how you react to it that matters." If you've ever played any sport in the world, you know that reaction is everything. How you hit the ball, respond to the tackle, shoot the puck or aim at the target determines your outcomes. Inside the game, a series of reactions to what's happening at that moment is the only way to play.

A client of mine, Tim, was working on a permit job. He was handed a bunch of details that showed that the person who had the gig before him didn't do a great job. He's dealing with pressure from investors, and the permitting has to be done right, and he's uncovering one problem after another. Then the company decides to acquire another business—adding this incredible workload of M&A (mergers and acquisitions) activity to my client's responsibility. He was working ridiculous hours. And I said to him, "Tim, how are you doing?"

He went on for about 10 minutes, outlining the chaos involved in his daily life. I listened.

After a pause, I said, "Okay, but how do you feel?"

"I've never slept better in my life," Tim said.

The shitstorm was raging all around him. But he was not the storm. His parts were not trying to protect him. Understanding the situation helped him to calmly address the situation—and he was 1,000% more effective because of it. He accessed a Self-energy, finding peace of mind in the middle of the maelstrom. He was capitalizing on chaos, not being ruled by it.

"I'm here to fix the company's problems," Tim told me. "But I'm not the company's problem. And these issues aren't a personal problem for me—they are just part of my job."

If you're in a sport and you're thinking about what the coach said last Wednesday, or you're imagining the hero's welcome that awaits you after you hit the home run, you're going to fail. Imagining yourself as the hero or a piece of shit isn't going to help you. You know why? You've already got too much on your mind.

When I played water polo, we would be in the middle of an incredibly tough match. We'd been swimming our guts out and then, BAM, the ball came my way. I saw the shot, right in front of me! At that precise moment, I can tell you exactly what I was thinking about:

Nothing.

That's right. I was in the game, and I was in myself. That ball needed to go in the net, and those bastards from Princeton or Penn

State were not going to stop me from doing what needed to be done! More importantly, I wasn't going to stop myself. There was no need and no time for contemplation—it was time for action. I grabbed that ball and rose up and shoved it past the goalie. I was neither the hero nor a piece of shit—I was playing the game, full out, 100% in the moment. Have you been there? You know that feeling?

Even if you never played water polo, or any sport at all, I suspect you have access to the feeling I'm trying to describe. Some call it "flow"—it's the place where your thoughts show up more freely, without hesitation, as you realize what needs to be done. And you do it!

The opposite of this feeling of Self-energy is when you're lost in thought. You're not bringing your whole Self to the game. You are preoccupied.

"Keep your eye on the ball" my coaches always told me. In the game of life, that means remaining true to your values and your vision for yourself. (We will explore your values and your own personal vision in the next chapter, where we look at how to apply these ideas and create new results).

You've heard the saying, "If you're a hammer, the whole world looks like a nail?" So many times, our parts react to the world the way that a hammer reacts. Our parts can't see other possibilities.

That was my experience—I had to hammer the nail, which was me. I saw myself as an error that needed to be eliminated. An incorrect line of code that needed to be deleted, and that meant ending my life.

> *If you are experiencing suicidal ideation, don't hesitate to reach out for help in the United States and Canada, Dial 988. This number, 988, has been designated as the Suicide and Crisis Lifeline.*
>
> *If you are in another country, please go online to find resources that can help.*

Luckily, as you can tell by the words on this page, my dangerous parts eventually led me away from self-harm. I found a way to help me see alternatives. Calming the parts helped me to see the whole. Calming that part helped me to *stay* whole. Along the way, here's what I discovered:

Fear turns us into hammers.

A hammer can be a useful tool or a destructive instrument. Maybe even a murder weapon. Be careful.

For the cowardly part, the hammer of fear is frozen in space and time. It's a tool that's not in use. Not helping anyone. Not healing anyone. Not even a nail. For other destructive parts, the hammer becomes a passive-aggressive tool for destruction. The hammer makes a mess when we don't know how to use it to build things. We all have fears—we all have hammers inside of us.

Don't fight the part of yourself that is bringing fear into your world. Use your tools and your parts in a way that creates progress. Create conversations, don't run from them, especially when that conversation can lead to self-discovery. Find the courage to move into the "fire of self-discovery," as the quote says in the first chapter. "It will not burn you; it will only burn what you are not."

Recognize that we all experience fear. Is it rational, or irrational? That distinction isn't useful. Emotions exist—can you accept that fact? From acknowledgement, recognize and appreciate what your parts are trying to tell you. Embrace the messenger, don't argue.

Notice what's really going on. Your parts are, by definition, only a part of you. These parts may cause you to behave a certain way (like an asshole, or a hammer, perhaps). But, inside of you, the whole is always greater than the sum of the parts it's made of. Returning to your whole Self—returning to that feeling—is the key.

Recognize that you always have other options. Speak to yourself with candor and compassion—it's the first step in showing up in that same spirit for your team and your organization.

It's time to play a new game. A game I had to learn, through my own personal journey of Self-discovery. I'm talking about "Self" with a capital S.

Because when we return to Self, we find clarity inside of chaos. We turn away from the oh-so-serious and detrimental negative self-talk, the strange loop that can lead us to very dark and unproductive places. With Self-energy, we discover a new way to show up. A new way to play the game. And, yes, "playfulness" is part of the clarity we must discover.

My friend and IFS instructor, Dr. Dave Lovas, is an IFS certified psychiatrist and professor at Dalhousie University in Nova Scotia. He says, "Parts have a piece of the truth, but only you (Self) has the whole truth."

To me, I liken IFS to a team. The team is made up of parts of you, instead of people that you lead. Like any team, it requires empathy, facilitation, listening, curiosity, and non-assholery. You're the leader, so your job is to make your parts feel valued and heard. That way, you can educate them with the whole truth and lead them to the best outcome for the system (you).

But don't get me wrong. Destructive leadership parts always exist—they never go away. (I'm guessing it's because not everyone has read my book?) For yourself, and for others: there is another way. Leadership means leading the team inside of you, so that you can lead your company as well.

Perception is reality, as you know. By relaxing our protector parts, we can open our perception to new possibilities. This openness is based on neuroscience: when we are anxious/stressed/afraid, our frontal lobe shuts down and we can't access our full abilities.

Consider the hockey player, asked to shoot 10 pucks from center ice into an unprotected and unobstructed goal. With no obstacles, the player is certain that she can hit 10 out of 10 into the back of the net. Easy, right? She's ready to go!

Now imagine that I have access to all of her money and tell her that if she misses one shot on goal, it's gone.

What percentage of the pucks do you think she will hit into the back of the net? Now she doesn't want to play—she's not sure she can make 100% of the shots. Why?

Maybe putting pressure on ourselves doesn't help improve performance.

Have you ever considered that the greatest athletes in the world are the ones who are able to quiet the parts of themselves that want to scream about the "Unbelievable pressure!!" Because, in my experience as an elite athlete I have discovered something. The thoughts surrounding the *pressure* of athletic competition are not useful at all.

So how can you access peak performance? By working with our parts, we can change our minds. That changes our perception and therefore, changes our reality—from chaos to clarity. Pressure exists; the elite just respond to it differently.

When our fear shuts us down from taking action, we don't always notice it. Until inaction prevents us from achieving our goals. When you don't ask that person out, you don't call that prospect, you don't explain why you deserve more equity, what happens? You learn the difference between action and regret.

When we align our minds with our goals, connections happen because our brain is subconsciously looking for them. Have you ever had resources show up even when you weren't actively searching and seeking something? I'm talking about people who can help you on your journey who suddenly show up and cross your path. Perhaps this book being in your hands right now is one such example of serendipity— what you really want and need, whether you are aware of it or not.

As hockey great Wayne Gretzky said, "You miss 100% of the shots you don't take." For people who are afraid of not being good enough, not being accepted, not being loved… they aren't taking shots on goal. And if you're wondering what kind of people live life like this, the answer is, all people. People like you and me. It's human nature for us to give up on what we want, as we settle for what we think we can get.

Don't look now but the puck is coming your way—are you ready to pursue your goals?

You know you can have almost anything in this world, if you don't talk yourself out of it first. That means you might need to quiet your parts and come back to your Self.

ASKING FOR HELP

Asking for advice is my best tip, my best motivational tool, my best suggestion for finding new solutions.

When you ask people who can help you achieve your goals for advice, you get valuable guidance that can take you over, around or through the chaos.

1. People love to feel like they are experts and that their advice matters.
2. People will give you advice and, because they gave you this advice, they want the advice to be "right"—in other words, valuable. This desire (to create valuable advice and to be seen as a worthwhile resource) can lead them to supporting your goals.

Asking for help is so easy to do and so powerful, especially for people who do it strategically. But you have to take the first step. You have to ask.

However, please remember: not everyone on this earth is a worthy resource. Asking everybody for help makes you look confused and/or lost, not strategic. Find the right person and ask the right question— you'll know it when you feel it. And if you don't, keep looking!

ACCESS THE SELF: WHY IT MATTERS

How do you know when you are accessing Self-energy?
Look for a feeling.

That's right. Self-energy is a personal experience, not an intellectual one. It is felt.

I describe that feeling as an internal calmness. A tranquility and groundedness—maybe even "playfulness?" The experience is one of deep calm and knowing, inside the storm that surrounds you. Here's a quick quiz to test your current state of mind:

1. Are you able to laugh at yourself and your circumstances?
2. Are you able to come up with creative solutions?
3. How spontaneous are you?

Consider the athletes you admire in team sports like soccer. During his prime, Messi was the master of unexpected and innovative solutions—blowing by players with a God-given gift of acceleration, to be sure. But Messi is a prime example of "thinking on your feet," quite literally. Perhaps no other modern athlete has the ability to react and respond with such a wide array of unique approaches to world-class competition. What does that look like, for you, in the game of life that you are playing?

When do you show up at your best, with a kind of child-like sense of wonder and discovery? Look at the talented troupe of performers on a show like *Whose Line is It Anyway?* These folks are living life at the fullest—coming up with ideas that are wild—and wildly entertaining! I'm not suggesting you bring enormous Styrofoam props into the conference room (head to YouTube if you don't know what I'm talking about). I'm saying that there's an element of improvisation in every career. Life is unscripted. Even if you live and die by rules and regulations, you still have the ability to show up in new ways.

Like boundaries and center lines on a highway: the rules keep us on the road. But where you take that road is really up to you, now isn't it?

A useful exercise includes recalling and describing that feeling when you were at your best. Some call it being "in the pocket" (my favorite), "flow" or "being in the zone." Recall a time when you felt that you were truly in Self.

1. Where were you?
2. What were you doing?
3. Who were you with?
4. How did you *feel?*

Now, phase II: step beyond your circumstances but stay with the memory.

Because where you are is not who you are. Indeed, you can be inside of stressful circumstances and feel completely at home, at peace and at one with your Self. Tim showed me that, and I've discovered this experience on countless occasions, both personally and with my clients.

We all have the capacity to return to Self. You know this. You feel this. So, stay with that feeling. Recall that time when you were at that place inside yourself where you were just... true. Where you were just being you.

Have you ever noticed that babies don't need therapy? Why is that?

You might say that it's because they don't have an awareness of all the chaos in the world. They are held and loved and fed and squeezed, so they don't know how bad life really is. Maybe you're right. But your reasoning is incomplete. Because babies are always and only an expression of Self. They just are. They are pure, innocent, and unencumbered. Playful and experimental, babies meet the world with wonder.

I'm not suggesting you go try on a diaper and face the world of work like a big baby (that would be weird).

I'm asking you to remember where you came from. Touch that place inside yourself that existed (and exists now) before you start to think of yourself, your circumstances, your life.

Who are you when you aren't on your mind?

Who are you when your parts aren't trying to protect you, shield you, or otherwise over-index on imagined threats and challenges? That is your Self.

Your parts are still there—you still have the ability to manage, to fight fires, to respond to the world of 10,000 things. But, from Self, you respond differently. You show up with all of your resources and your insights and your wisdom, ready to play. Flexibility is there, even as you consider the rules and regulations that define the edges of the game.

As human beings, we are all built to be really good at two things:

1. **Making up shit that we think we need to fix, figure out, defend or overcome.** Here, we descend into the world of worry, where our parts come to the rescue. Our imagination is in hyper-drive. But really we are going nowhere, fast.

2. **Getting shit done.** Taking action to solve real problems, accessing our true nature (Self) and letting our parts become a useful part of the whole is always a possibility. We can show up differently, even when our circumstances haven't changed, and *get shit done.*

Reflect on your own experience. Have you ever had a super-stressful series of events, and yet you took it all in stride? In spite of pressures and challenges, you were getting shit done? Compare that to the overwhelming time you couldn't find your car keys, and you started sweating, scrambling and screaming… only to find out that they were in your blue jacket?

Hold on a second… Let me apologize to my wife and thank her for helping me to find my keys.

OK, I'm back. Consider the feeling of Self-energy from outside your circumstances. Outside your relationships. Outside of your job title. And look at the people who are trying to help you. These kind souls are your team members. They want you to find victory in the Capitalizing on Chaos Game.

WHERE TO LOOK?

Finding Self is not an external investigation or an internet search. It's easier to access than Google. You just have to look inside. Because that's where you will find your Self! And not to get too Zen on you, but you just might find what is seeking you. I'm talking about the part of life that's trying to come through you.

Maybe that's a new business. A new product design. A new way of mining in the Northwest Territories. Or perhaps it's a song, a poem... maybe even a book. Life takes many shapes and leads us to many interesting places. Where does your Self want to go?

NOTICE WHAT'S AVAILABLE

Self-energy is not selfish energy. It's the feeling when we are living life, and life is living through us, doesn't have a value-judgment label. The feeling is one without attachment, where we are aware of possibilities not tied to outcomes. Being human is nothing more and nothing less than being who you are.

Jeanette Bronée is the author of *The Self-Care Mindset*. She writes, "Self-care is the strongest and most resilient emotion that drives us. It keeps us aligned with our ethics, hopes, and dreams. We often hear that love is the strongest emotion, but I believe that care is... we choose the company we want to work for, and the people we enjoy working with, because we care about the same things. That's how we create change and impact together. The future of work is about CARE." That caring intention isn't selfish. In fact, in great organizations, it's shared!

Dr. Schwartz, the founder of IFS therapy, describes aspects of Self-Energy. There are eight P's and 5 c's that make up the Self. As you reflect on your own experience, when you are truly at your best, which of these words and characteristics show up for you?

We are all unique individuals, yet we share common characteristics. Regardless of race, gender, education or experience, there's something that unites us. It's called "human nature." We all possess the ability to love, to fear, to crave, to antagonize, to cherish, and more, each according to our own appetites and emotional experiences. But these qualities are part of the human experience. We are all made up of many parts, and embracing our parts makes us whole.

Are you ready to embrace being human, and fall in love with your Self? It's not selfish, self-serving or anything like that. Returning to Self is the healthiest thing you will ever do! Trust me—the discovery literally saved my life.

When we return to Self we have access to all of these P and C qualities. Our parts are still there, ready to go on the next mission—but they are calmer. Quieter. More useful.

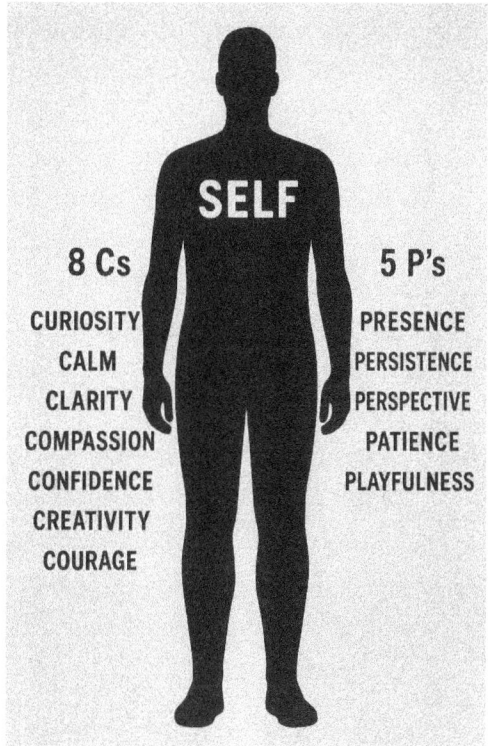

SELF

8 Cs	5 P's
CURIOSITY	PRESENCE
CALM	PERSISTENCE
CLARITY	PERSPECTIVE
COMPASSION	PATIENCE
CONFIDENCE	PLAYFULNESS
CREATIVITY	
COURAGE	

Just as all humans are born with five fingers on a hand, these Self-energy qualities are part of who we are. It's just that sometimes our parts won't allow us to see that fact.

In my work with hundreds of clients, as well as what I have seen in my own experience: We are never more than one thought away from innate mental health.

On the surface that might seem crazy, or glib. But hear me out on this. Consider your own experience as well -and reflect on these words from Shakespeare's *Hamlet*:

"There is nothing either good or bad in this world, but thinking makes it so."

The distance between chaos and compassion is the size of a thought.

Have you ever met an asshole and then… you find out he's really not all that bad? Have you ever thought that a project would never come in on time and then, it does? Have you ever viewed a situation as chaotic, but with a small shift you see the way forward with utter clarity?

Suicide to Self: it was one thought away. True, there was an internal dialogue and exploration inside that thought, but that initial thought… the realization that killing myself was not the only choice. Wow. For the first time, I felt the power of Self-energy. It felt like a "What if…?" exploration, and it led me to a new life. Namely, a life where I got to be alive. From there, gratitude, peace… and a strong desire to share these ideas with all who wish to rise above the parts that keep us from being whole.

How big is a problem when it's not on your mind?

I had this misconception, early on in my coaching journey, that if I could get to Self, I would become… enlightened, somehow. Like a monk on a mountaintop. I would be one of maybe three people in the world who had achieved Zen, or Nirvana, or whatever. I would have nothing on my mind! I would achieve bliss, or ignorance, or both!

Then I remembered the words of Brittney Spears. "I'm addicted to you, don't you know that you're toxic?" As you can tell from this reference, the ignorance was starting to overcome me! That line reflected my relationship with suicidal ideation. But nevertheless, I realized I had to break the addiction. I had to break away from the toxic—the chaos—and return to myself.

Britney was right. But mine was not a "poison paradise"—more like a suicidal prison. As I escaped, I was certain that the quest would help me to transcend emotion, allowing me to leave behind the painful and suicidal ideations that were haunting me. I imagined I would be able to float through life in some state of Zen-like trance, where nothing triggered me.

The fact is that disappointment didn't disappear.

Reacting to people, places and things still happened. And thank God it did—because it meant I was human. At the end of the day, I didn't want to be someone else. I wanted to be me. I wanted to find myself. I wanted to get back to the guy who was hidden inside the suicidal impulses. I knew he was in there.

The difference I discovered wasn't inside my circumstances. The change was inside of me. I stopped chasing career goals and numbers in my bank account. I got clear on what really mattered—and I'll share more on that journey in the next chapter.

LEARNING TO REBOUND

My ambitions and goals didn't go away. I still wanted things, and sometimes those things didn't work out. Just as some days it rains, and some days the sun shines, I found myself faced with different circumstances. When I returned to Self, I started reaching for an umbrella on those rainy days, instead of crying about the storm clouds. "You are the sky," Buddhist teacher, nun & author, Pema Chödrön says. "Everything else is just weather."

Just as rain is impersonal (it's not the product of a malevolent spirit peeing on the world, it's just water in the air!) I wondered if my reaction could be the same. In other words, impersonal. The universe wasn't out to get me. I just needed to remember to grab an umbrella. I could even have my parts help me to find the umbrella! My manager parts were useful, not harmful, when I came to see new pathways and new ideas.

I remembered the words of Marcus Aurelius, the great Roman emperor, who said, "You always own the option of not having an opinion." When I come back to Self, I find I don't have as many opinions.

Want to know what freedom feels like? It's not having as many opinions. When I stop feeling attacked, I'm able to take new action. When I stop being defensive, I see new opportunities. Especially when I stop attacking myself, the battle is already won.

When I stop creating stories about who I am, what I'm worth, and whether or not I'm a decent person, I reframe my internal chaos.

Is it your boss's behavior, or your stories around it, that are causing you harm?

Returning to Self, I learned, is what helps you to bounce back more quickly. You know that not every shot is going to go into the goal. What if I stopped beating myself up after every missed opportunity or situation that didn't go my way? After all, I started to realize, sometimes things didn't go the way I wanted—and sometimes, they actually turned out *better* than what I had imagined!

Sunny Strasburg, one of my favorite teachers and spiritual guides, shares her take on the Chödrön quote from the prior page. She says, "Self is the sky, your parts are the weather." I've learned to love all four seasons and accept whatever weather I find. How about you?

How you rebound determines your outcome, in any game. Disappointed? Bounce back. Feeling left out? Bounce back. Thinking that you are a piece of shit? Hey, what else could this mean?! Bounce back! Drop the story you're telling yourself. Ask your parts to calm down. Bring Self-energy to the situation!

You can give Self-energy to your parts, when times are tough— some call this self-care. You can choose your reaction in any and every scenario.

Consider your options. You can interpret events in the worst possible way (I have a lot of expertise in this area). But I have also discovered you also interpret events in a way that's generous and compassionate, where your parts are not screaming and freaking out and telling you to take your own life. What do you think will help you most, as you face chaos?

The way you win is simple: you return to your Self. Not your self-talk. Your Self. Your true and authentic Self—accessing the genius and miracles that are inside of you.

Now you may think that saying you are made of genius and miracles is bullshit. I get it. But you are more than just flesh and blood.

Look, I don't need to pump you up—you already bought the book. So instead of flattery let me give you honesty.

The fact that you are accessing these words is a modern miracle. From the odds against your conception and birth to your triumphs over disease, puberty, pandemics and politics, your very existence is an absolutely infinite series of possibilities and coincidences. Isn't life kind of amazing, when you think about it?

In this regard, I call you a miracle. I don't mean "miracle" in a religious context, I mean that you are a modern miracle that defies science and mathematics, because you are a nearly infinite expression of unique possibility.

Similarly, you have the ability to access genius. Don't believe me? Let me ask you if you have ever had a brilliant idea show up from out of nowhere? Ever had someone say to you, "Wow—that's genius!" Or have you said it to yourself, or to someone else?

Isn't it interesting to notice that ideas always seem to show up out of nowhere? Because, for all our research into the nuances of the human brain, scientists still can't tell us where ideas come from. From nowhere to somewhere. Think about that for a second.

From nowhere to somewhere: that's exactly how this book was created! Inside Self-energy, we bring the formless into form. We create designs, business plans, org charts, relationships, families and investment opportunities. All of the things that you see in the world were once just passing thoughts!

That car that just drove by your apartment building? Started as an idea. Same for your apartment building. The clothes you are wearing. The movie you just watched. From something to nothing. Self-energy is very powerful, indeed—it's the creative force behind life itself!

Maybe it might be useful to learn more about how to harness its power—and capitalize on chaos?

Ever hear a little kid say something brilliant, or surprising? Ever have an employee, or someone you've just met, deliver an insight that makes you say, "Wow!"

Just as chaos exists, so does genius. How can people and organizations get more of that—more genius? The first step is observation. Be aware that we all have the ability to tap into genius. Maybe you won't go out and cure cancer, but you have the capacity inside of you, right now, to make a difference in this world. Starting by making a difference to yourself.

Recognize that genius exists inside of you. See that your very existence is a miracle. The fact that you have lived the life you have led and experienced the challenges you have overcome is an absolute mountain of coincidences that defies logic and understanding—another word for a miracle.

And even if words like genius and miracle don't feel like a fit for you, try this on for size: inside your true Self are capacities and capabilities that go beyond your self-imposed limitations, and the boundaries that your parts have made up.

New possibilities always exist. Self-energy helps us to see new ways of playing the game of life. And when we see new ways to play, we discover new ways to win. Hardship and difficulty will never go away—but neither does your genius. Your ability to solve real problems and figure things out and face circumstances with renewed courage and capacity always exists—even inside of chaos.

Self-energy is the answer. And it's been there for you this whole time. Access your Self, and you discover a playfulness and possibility that just might change your life.

BREAKDOWN TO BREAK THROUGH

1. **Rediscover Your Playfulness:** Embrace a sense of playfulness at work by reconnecting with your inner Self. This doesn't mean literal play but adopting a mindset that allows you to engage with tasks and challenges in a more relaxed and enjoyable manner.
2. **Access Self-Energy:** Remember that your natural state of calm and clarity is always available. When you approach work from this place of inner peace, you can transform challenges into opportunities for growth and creativity.

3. **Embrace Compassion Over Criticism:** Shift from self-criticism to self-compassion. Instead of berating yourself, treat yourself with kindness and understanding. This shift can lead to more productive and less stressful work experiences.

4. **Act From the Present Moment:** Connecting to Self can help you to focus on the task at hand without being bogged down by past failures or future anxieties. Like being "in the zone" during a sport, fully engaging in the present moment can lead to better performance and satisfaction.

EXPLORATIONS

1. **Personal Reflection**: Can you recall a time when a stressful situation suddenly felt more manageable or even enjoyable? What changed in your mindset or approach that allowed you to experience this shift?

2. **Exploring Inner States**: How does accessing a sense of playfulness, curiosity or calm affect your performance and interactions at work? How might this approach help you deal with current challenges? How would accessing these states impact your leadership?

3. **Bravery in Leadership**: Have you ever noticed any personal fears or behaviors that might be holding you back from being a more effective leader? How could embracing a more compassionate and curious mindset change your approach to these situations?

4. **Feedback and Growth**: In what ways could you support others in finding their own sense of play, curiosity and Self-energy at work? How might encouraging this perspective help reduce conflict and foster a more positive work environment?

CHAPTER 12

EXPLORING THE SELF

> *"Everything that irritates us about others can lead us to an understanding of ourselves."*
>
> — CARL JUNG, FOREFATHER OF MODERN PSYCHOLOGY

I was wearing a mask.

I'd spent my life craving recognition and validation, from water polo, school, and my parents. Validation was my survival strategy. The mask I wore for the outside world was called, "Reliable Rob."

I had no idea who I was under that mask. And I wore it so long, I convinced myself, "This is me."

By now you know that our parts are not exactly real people. These parts are archetypes, or amalgams (characterizations made up of more than one person). The Destructive Six—the six types of toxic leaders identified in the Swedish study—are façades. Masks. Parts. Of course, if you work for one of these assholes, the punishment and frustration can feel very real. But what if those feelings didn't have to rule your day? What if you can find compassion inside of chaos? In my experience, that's the only way through it.

Returning to Self helps you to access new resources—to find new ways of looking at the same old problems. While your board chair may not be willing to change, you can always change how you show up. And how you show up, at work, at home, and for yourself: that's what creates your world.

We focus so much on our externals—our masks—when what really matters is where we are on the inside. Believe me, I know. My externals looked good. But on the inside, I wanted to end it all.

Exploring Self means removing the mask and stepping into who we really are. But why would you want to do that? What's the benefit of exploring who you really are—instead of trying to live up to a persona that you've created?

First of all, let me ask you a question: How's that mask thing working out for you?

Do you ever stop and wonder, "Is this all there is?" Who am I trying to be? Do you ever find yourself feeling exhausted, or fake, or both?

Unmasked Self-energy is an always-available resource. A powerful resource that never runs out, strengthening your ability to get things done. But in order to reach that place, you have to run a little experiment.

STEP 1: ACCESSING YOUR VALUES

Researchers at Stanford University wanted to discover ways to help stressed-out college students. So, prior to winter break, they took a group of students and asked them to write in journals over the holidays. Pretty simple, right?

But for a select group of students, they gave them a more detailed assignment. They asked them to write about their *values*. More specifically, they asked them to write about how they saw their values expressed in everyday life. These students identified examples and evidence of their values, in their actions and daily experiences.

The results of the experiment stunned the scientists who created it. That's according to Kelly McGonigal, the Stanford psychologist who wrote about it in *The Upside of Stress*. In her book, she writes how the values group experienced better health than the control group (the ones that just journaled, without any direction or purpose). But that was just the tip of the iceberg.

Surprisingly, the values group exhibited greater resilience, a sense of camaraderie and support, improved health and even improved grades!

Why?

McGonigal says,

> *Writing about personal values makes people feel more powerful, in control, proud and strong. It also makes them feel more loving, connected and empathetic toward others. It increases pain tolerance, enhances self-control and reduces unhelpful rumination after a stressful experience.*

This exercise has been repeated in various scenarios, both in and out of academic environments. Researchers call it a *self-affirmation* exercise—a powerful tool in the journey back to Self. In the long term, "writing about values has been shown to boost GPAs, reduce doctor visits, improve mental health, and help with everything from weight loss to quitting smoking and reducing problem drinking," McGonigal writes.

Seems to be a lot of value in writing about your values. In Ontario, at the University of Waterloo, researchers gave out wristbands with a simple message: "Remember Your Values." Your values are the first step in self-affirmation—the journey back to Self.

"When self-affirmed, individuals feel as though the task of proving their worth, both to themselves and to others, is 'settled.' As a consequence, they can focus on other salient [meaningful] demands in the situation beyond ego protection." That's according to psychologists Sherman and Cohen, who did a multi-year study on the repeated results of various examples of the values experiment. They shared their findings in an article entitled, *Psychology of Self-Defense: Self-Affirmation Theory*.

Connecting to your values, via evidence-based journaling, can help you to take positive action—calming your parts, and seeing your Self in a new light—avoiding procrastination and viewing adversity as temporary (which is just a small part of the positive results that showed up for the participants). In essence, people who connect with their personal values via journaling see themselves as people who can conquer challenges—resilient, resourceful, and strong. These sentiments reflect Self-energy. A mindset shift towards our values can calm our parts, greatly reducing asshole behavior.

Science says our values can bring us back to Self.

In fact, people who did this values-exploration experiment, writing about how they see their values in evidence, and doing it just one time for 10 minutes, displayed traits of positive change (resilience, resourcefulness, and a renewed sense of capacity—even improved health) months after the writing period took place.

Can it really be as simple as finding yourself, in about 10 minutes? Science says, "yes"—will you say yes, and take 10 minutes to write about how you see your values, in evidence, in your everyday life?

EXAMPLES of VALUES			
Family	Integrity	Patience	Forgiveness
Honesty	Compassion	Wisdom	Excellence
Courage	Responsibility	Generosity	Health
Trust	Fairness	Harmony	Adventure
Friendship	Freedom	Learning	Loyalty
Love	Accountability	Innovation	Reliability
Creativity	Gratitude	Dignity	Serenity
Justice	Empathy	Achievement	Peace
Kindness	Humility	Ambition	Service
Authenticity	Self-discipline	Sustainability	Open-mindedness
Growth	Balance	Equality	Family
Security	Tolerance	Respect	Independence

Take ten minutes and write your answers. The journey to Self-discovery has begun.

STEP 2: FIND SUPPORT

Christina, my coaching client, was worried.

A high achiever, her constant perfectionist tendencies were driving her team insane. She was miserable, working herself into a hole—some might say, "a-hole"—and she couldn't find a way out. Her team's performance was poor, their work sub-par, infighting was frequent, and the amount of conflict was rising. The cycle kept repeating itself —the very definition of burnout. I took time to let Christina share her situation. And I listened, without judgment—taking in everything that she was experiencing.

Notice that I didn't get caught up in what she was saying about her team, agreeing with her and saying, "Yeah, your team sucks! Let's dive into a decision matrix to see who you need to fire and then we will move on to making sure you have the right butts in the right seats!" I didn't say, "Why aren't people doing their jobs, Christina?" I didn't try to manage or fix the situation in any way. Her manager parts were already working triple-overtime to try and sort out her frustrations and the team's poor performance. Was she really in a place where a decision matrix—a reminder of her shortcomings as well as the failings of her team—would be useful? No. Because wise counsel at the wrong time isn't very wise at all. And that approach is definitely not good coaching.

It didn't make sense to jump onto the pile and add more managerial thinking—why pour gasoline on a fire? Something else showed up for me. What if my manager parts didn't need to be a part of the conversation? I remembered my values. And one of the things I valued was Christina—my client. I also value empathy.

I value service—always looking towards what will help my clients most. I've been in some pretty dark places, and I was fortunate to have coaches around me who were willing to help. Could I do the same for Christina?

A part of Christina was a scared little girl. Always trying to do the right thing, and now she was wondering if she had the strength to keep going. I knew that same scared part inside myself. She was dealing with massive leadership challenges, disappointment, conflict... in a word, chaos. And she had an absolute fear that this shit was going to cost her her career.

"Christina," I said to her, "I can see how hard you work."

I paused. It wasn't an offhand remark, or small talk. It was acknowledgement.

The remark was unexpected. It stopped her in her tracks. She cocked her head to the side, as if I had suddenly started speaking fluent Albanian. I saw that she didn't need a translator—the unexpected words were ones that she understood. She just hadn't heard them, in quite the same way, before.

I spoke simply and slowly. "I see how much you care."

Christina burst into tears.

When our parts release, and Self-energy arrives, it can often be accompanied by tears. Or laughter. Or silence. Remember how Self-energy is a feeling? A feeling that brings you back to yourself? Christina's journey had just begun.

STEP 3: MEETING YOUR SELF FOR THE FIRST TIME

Strategies and tactics don't matter until Self-energy is there to receive new ideas. Otherwise, your parts keep on defending you, blocking insight and inadvertently defending the status quo. Christina began to see, from a calmer place and a safer space, that her team wasn't performing because she wasn't allowing it. People didn't "step up and do things" because she wasn't letting them. She wasn't giving people a chance.

Did I need to point that out to her? No. In fact, I don't recall that I could even see the challenge until she discovered it for herself. Or should I say, *from* her Self. Her team was afraid of making mistakes, and so was Christina. From common ground, she began to discover uncommon results.

In my experience, coaching is a supportive, focused, professional conversation that helps you to discover what was there all along. Coaching, at its core, is encouragement. A gentle reminder that your Self-energy is always there. Always available. Always ready to wrap you in a feeling that says, "Yes, you can."

Christina's discovery reminded me of Roald Amundsen, the explorer who discovered the South Pole, way back in 1911. He was the first explorer to discover the Pole—but think about it: the South Pole had always been there.

He just needed to reach it—and see it for himself. That's how discoveries work.

Christina knew that if she told her troubles to her friends, her friends would just agree with her. They would do what good friends do: jump on board and trash Christina's lousy employees. Christina might feel supported. But would she be making progress?

The coach sees that something more than agreement is needed when dealing with chaos. The ability to compassionately and gently pierce the armor of the parts, in the spirit of saying what will help most, is the role of the coach.

Respectfully disagreeing is part of the conversation, without judgment, so that curiosity drives the conversation. I didn't have an opinion or tactic or strategy that Christina hadn't considered yet. Christina knew her world and her needs much better than I did. If I saw something that might help, I would share it—and that's what I did. I saw that she needed to be seen. She needed to be heard. She needed her pain to be held in a space without judgment or prescription, so that she could find the strength that was already inside of her.

Remember, Christina was an executive leader with a lifetime of professional experience—it would be the purest form of bullshit for me to believe I knew some managerial tactics that she did not. Many of my clients come from industries that I have never worked in, with expertise that I don't share. How, you may wonder, is it possible that I can be their coach?

Consider this question: do you have to be an Olympic-level swimmer in order to coach someone to be a better swimmer?

The answer, of course, is no. Why is that?

Of course, you have to know how to swim. But beyond that, what really matters—the real source of the coach's power—is perspective. It is your ability to see the swimmer in the pool that allows you to offer new insight. From the deck of the pool, the coach has what no swimmer can ever possess: an outside perspective.

Let's test your coaching instincts further. Is it more useful to identify what someone is lacking, confronting that person with their faults and flaws—or is it better to start by catching someone doing something right?

I knew that Christina's answers were going to come from one place and one place only: inside of her Self. My job wasn't to offer tips and techniques—my job was to help her get back to the personal power that was waiting for her, ready to open her up to new ideas, and a world without fear or the micro-management tactics that her parts had made up.

Beyond tips, and tricks, I could see what was true. And the truth that I saw was that she had what she needed, if she could just get back to herself. Plus, have you ever tried to offer tips and tricks when someone is deep into a really stressful situation? It's like having a friend come to you and tell you about his impending divorce, and you say, "There's other fish in the sea! Let me show you some dating apps and teach you how to create a really snazzy online profile!" Can you imagine? Do you want to get punched in the throat? Offering advice in the midst of the dark times is the last thing somebody needs. Trying to be a guru with all the answers when people are hurting is the opposite of helping. I don't play that game.

I've said it before, but it bears repeating. Human beings are really good at making shit up, creating stress and finding things to worry about. But we are even better at solving real problems—especially when we do so from a place of Self-energy. That discovery was what Christina was missing—and what we uncovered, together.

From Self-energy, Christina was open to new ideas—because fear wasn't blocking her options. We explored accountability and empowerment—not from the standpoint of a list of to-dos that I offered her. She went from completely frozen with frustration to a new place—a place of exploration. Christina discovered something that she hadn't seen before. Just like Amundsen did in 1911, when he found what had always been there.

> "We shall not cease from exploration, and the end of all our exploring will be to arrive where we started, and know the place for the first time."
>
> — T. S. ELIOT, LITTLE GIDDING

Your parts want to help you. But if you fight those parts—and dumping advice on someone who's hurting is another way to start a fight—your parts become stronger. More entrenched. Less useful. Fear rules the day and takes over the conversation. The funny thing is that the opposite of fear isn't courage. It's love.

That's right. What would happen if you fell in love with your parts?

It's a crazy construct, I know, but consider the idea for a moment. If you love your parts, you wouldn't fight with them or try to wrestle with your perceived shortcomings. Your parts are not what make you incomplete. Your parts are what complete you. Chaos to clarity begins with an embrace.

Self-energy, combined with your parts, is what allows all of us to function in the world. Our ability to engage with self-energy is directly proportional to the amount of ease, grace and innovation we are able to bring to any situation.

My speaker coach, who helped me with my TEDx talk in Japan, does an exercise called "Soul on Sole." She asked me to write down what I wanted to create in my TEDx talk—but she suggested that I write the words on the soles of my feet! Sounds crazy, right? But I was already speaking at a Japanese Noh Theater—which doesn't mean it was not a theater. "Noh" is a stylized type of theater where the actors wear masks.

The Japanese who frequent Noh Theater recognize the stage as a sacred space. So, all who step onto the stage must do so with specialized socks, called "tabi," because your feet will be touching the god of theater, the god that lives inside the stage. Instead of laughing at this practice, like some uninformed Canadian, I became a student of the culture and custom around Noh. That's why, when you watch my TEDx talk, you'll see me wearing tabi socks in the video! But what you can't see is that I have written one word on each foot: "Self-energy" and "Love." Because that's what I wanted to stand on, as I took that stage. I wanted to send love out to the audience, because—if they have chaos in their lives, I know that love is what they need. Love is always the antidote. And accessing that love, for me, means stepping into Self-energy.

I don't know if you want to take a sharpie and start putting words on your feet. Still, I am glad I had the experience. Perhaps it's worthwhile to ask: What are you standing on? What do you want to step into? What stage are you seeking, and can you allow self-energy to help you to get there?

Self-energy can take you from catastrophe to compassion. In a sense, Self-energy helps you to love yourself. As you can only give to others what you already possess, finding kindness for all of your parts can help you to bounce back from the chaos.

Separate yourself from your circumstances. Recognize that you are the thinker, not the thought. Recognize that your CEO/investor/board chair is not an asshole, but their parts are making it look like that's the case. Don't confuse identity with behavior, and you'll start to see new ways to respond. And for your own behavior that you might regret, remember, sometimes our parts can make choices for us.

What if your action was a choice (it always is), not a mistake? What if the behavior came from a part of you, but it did not define you? The past reminds us; it does not define us.

Whatever choices you made in the past, even if that choice was toxic or chaotic, you did so with the best thinking you had at the time. Knowing what you knew then, you did what you did. In fact, anyone else with the same life experience and knowledge that you had might have done the same thing.

Choices happen. Choices, not mistakes. The behavior came from your parts. And, as Maya Angelou says, when people know better they do better.

Now you know that some separation (from your parts and from your past) can bring healing. After all, the past is fixed—you can't change it. Luckily for you, the past does not create the future. The future always comes from one place and one place only: that's right now.

While the past may influence you, it doesn't determine your future. Your parts will try to convince you otherwise, but remember: you can always choose differently.

You can choose to fall in love with your past. I have.

As wild and as foolish and as self-destructive as my journey once was, I could never be the person I am today without my entire lifetime of experiences. Embracing the whole and the parts, I discover that I can give to others what I have needed most: a second chance.

True, I can never go back to jobs that didn't work out, or revisit relationships that have ended. I can't resurrect the people close to me that I have lost. But I can always bring new life to the way I show up, right now. Because of my past, or in spite of it, I move forward towards personal freedom with every moment of every day. And I help my clients to do the same.

Because a life well-lived isn't something that's reserved for other folks. Falling in love with life is what Self-energy has to offer—as we connect and express our values, we discover what life really has in store for us. And it's not just a pile of chaos!

For me, I had to leave my job in heavy industry in order to find myself. I dropped my six-figure salary without a plan for the future. You may wonder, how could you do that, Rob?

All I can say is, I had a feeling. A feeling that came from a place of inner peace, and a desire for discovery. A discovery that I made, on that beach, with the two guys selling stuff out of a van. When my wife and I took a walk on the beach, I had the strangest feeling. There was a part of me that said, "Wow—I would love to do this!"

And another part of me said, "I will never let you do this!"

But when both of those parts settled, and I came back to Self, I realized something. Settling my parts allowed me to step outside of the expectations that my parents had for me. Thoughts like, "You have to live in the US, or Canada!" were replaced with a new truth. Namely, that lots of people live in lots of different places. There's no "one size fits all"—or one country is the only place where you can live. Where you start is not where you have to stay.

Similarly, I didn't have to work as an engineer. I knew that if coaching and Costa Rica didn't work out, I could always return to engineering. Instead of the lie that I was "losing everything" that catastrophic thinking gave way to clarity. In reality, I had choices and options!

So, I left my job, dove deep into coaching. My wife and I moved to Costa Rica.

In order to make that move, I had to realize (and internalize) several key ideas:

1. There are a lot of ways to make money. Engineering is one of them. So is coaching.
2. I could do what I thought I had to do. Or I could do what I love to do. I had choices. And those choices could change.

3. I needed to come back to my Self in order to understand what I really wanted—not just what I had been told was "acceptable" or "possible."

4. If I made a choice that didn't work out, I didn't have to waste time labeling it as a "mistake." I could simply make another choice. That was freedom—and I wanted to experience it!

Today, many of my clients wonder if they are in the right place. The right venture. The right career path. These concerns come to all of us, at varying degrees—and I can definitely relate. Do you feel a sense of freedom? Of possibility? Or something else?

My life and my choices are my own, just as it is for you and your path. Costa Rica isn't for everybody—I get that.

Second chances are always available. Reinvention is waiting for you. Maybe you don't have to pack up for Central America in order to find that out. But if you do choose to make a change, know that I support you. What would life look like for you, away from all the chaos? From a place of calm and clarity, what would you do? And how would your organization change?

By now I hope you realize that chaos isn't just a way of describing the unexpected or unpredictable in life and nature. Sometimes, chaos is a state of mind. And you don't have to go to that state if you don't want to.

I encourage you to find your path by experiencing the feelings that inspire you, that make you say, "Wow!" You never know what ideas might come to you when you're looking at two dudes who live out of a Volkswagen bus! Inspiration strikes in unusual and unexpected ways—reminding us that we can discover a feeling of expansion and possibility, regardless of our circumstances. Come back to Self, and you are embracing the whole. Not hiding behind a mask. Beyond your fears, and just past the lies your parts have told you, is your true Self. That possibility is always here, waiting for you.

BREAKDOWN TO BREAK THROUGH

1. **Unmasking the Self**: Removing the masks we wear to conform to external expectations means uncovering our genuine selves. Living behind a façade, like "Reliable Rob," can lead to feelings of exhaustion and disconnection… and worse.

2. **The Power of Self-Awareness**: Both IFS therapy and Jungian concepts highlight the significance of returning to our core Self. By accessing and acknowledging our internal values and needs, we can tap into a powerful, always-available resource that enhances our resilience and capacity to handle challenges.

3. **Value-Based Journaling**: Writing about personal values and observing how they manifest in daily life has been shown to improve resilience, health, and overall well-being. This self-affirmation practice helps shift focus from ego protection to meaningful actions, fostering a stronger connection with the Self. A worthy exploration is *The Shadow Work Journal* by Keila Shaheen. This runaway best-seller sold over 20 million copies, and it all started with Keila's videos on TikTok. Shaheen provides prompts and guidance for a productive journaling experience—helping people to transcend their shadows and journey towards deeper self-awareness and inner peace. Does that seem a little touchy-feely for your office? All I can say is: don't knock it till you try it. Self-exploration is a useful tool, if you are willing to use it!

4. **Coaching from Self-Energy**: Effective coaching involves guiding individuals back to their Self-energy rather than imposing external strategies. By seeing clients for who they truly are and helping them connect with their inner strengths, coaches can facilitate deeper insights and sustainable growth.

EXPLORATIONS

1. Can you recall a time when you felt like you were wearing a mask at work? How did it affect your well-being and performance? How might reconnecting with your core values change this experience?
2. What did you discover when you went through the Self-Affirmation exercise?
3. Reflecting on recent challenges at work, how have you managed to stay true to yourself? What strategies have helped you maintain your peace of mind, and how could focusing on your values further support you?
4. What role can a shared focus on values play in creating a more supportive and resilient work environment? How is your organization fostering this approach, if at all?

CHAPTER 13

FROM CHAOS TO CLARITY

FINDING NEW GROWTH

> "You can't really help others until you've helped yourself first."
>
> — JUNO TEMPLE, ACTRESS (KEELEY JONES ON TED LASSO)
>
> _____
>
> "The more we give away, the more is given to us."
>
> — WAYNE DYER, BEST-SELLING AUTHOR OF THE POWER OF INTENTION, YOUR ERRONEOUS ZONES, AND OVER 38 OTHER BOOKS

When you are 90 years old, and you look back on your life, what will you see? What will you remember? What did you create?

Creating a life that makes you say, "Wow!" is all about the now. Now is the time to step into Self, with trust and curiosity, and explore what's really waiting for you. Want to grow your organization? Interested in putting a stop to toxic leadership? Curious to build an environment where employees are engaged, not overwhelmed? Start on the inside. Start by finding your true Self and helping others to do the same.

Creating a new future for yourself, your team, and your organization is an inside job. When's the right time to capitalize on chaos, you may wonder?

Change always starts with… right now. As the Chinese proverb says, "The best time to plant a tree was twenty years ago. The second best time is now."

When I ask my clients to consider what their future self will find, it's surprising to me what I hear.

People have different dreams. Often, they are not about changing the whole world but just changing their own world. Can you relate? A client wants to be the best mom, to help her kids feel a certain way (confident and independent) as they grow up. Others want to start a business, help the homeless, or explore their faith and their spirituality. There's no value judgment on your values. So, whatever would make you say, "Wow!" makes me say "Wow!" too.

Have you ever noticed that even small miracles are still… miracles? Showing up differently at work and being more engaged may seem like an impossible dream or a minor miracle. But I have seen—for myself and my clients—that you can always show up differently. You don't have to be ruled by your parts, your past, your fears, or what looks like chaos.

Are you proud of what you did at the end of the day? Did you take some chances and show up for the people you cared about? Did you live your values?

I wonder about taking that small step today, that could help point you in the right direction—a direction that brings you back to who you were always meant to be.

There's a feeling of expansion, and growth inside that movement. The growth can be professional, personal and even spiritual (if you choose to look in that direction).

When we step away from chaos, we find ourselves creating a new kind of legacy.

Legacy means living a life that is true to who you are—not spraying insecurity into the cosmos—and transferring those insights to those around you.

When you are true to yourself, you are offering the world who you really are —a legacy we all need to embrace. When your contribution aligns with your values, your parts engage with the whole. And, in much the same way, you will engage with the whole of your organization. Your community. Your family. Your world.

We don't have to make billions of dollars or lead millions of people in order to find fulfillment, peace, and joy. We don't need titles and numbers in our bank accounts in order to say, "Hell yeah! That was awesome!" There are many things in this life that don't have a price tag, including joy, collaboration, friendships, and yes, even love. We fool ourselves into chasing achievement in all its external forms, when inner peace is, well... inside. (That's what "inner" means!)

Five years ago, I was living in Edmonton, in western Canada. I was working in heavy industry and feeling heavily depressed. Suicidal thoughts haunted me. I didn't have Winston, or much of anything that brought me joy.

I was wondering if I actually loved my beautiful wife.

Mbalia is her name, and she is my world. But at this time, there was a dark cloud inside my world. The cloud, like a thick fog, was keeping me from seeing her light. The thoughts that looked so solid and real were an illusion, but I couldn't see it yet—and I could not find my way back to Self.

I was so deep into "protection mode." My parts had clouded my thinking. My muddled thought process was keeping me from even trying at anything in work, because if I tried hard, what was going to happen? I didn't know, but my parts convinced me that it wouldn't be good. It couldn't be good. Because I was no good.

When you feel like whale shit (that would be the lowest thing on the bottom of the ocean), how can you really express love for your spouse? Your career? Your life?

Keep your head down, I thought. *Keep working, just keep moving forward… you piece of shit.* Yes, I talked to myself like that—and believe me, that's the edited and nice version of my inner monologue. Keep your head down, just keep going—like a damn zombie!

But I didn't want to live like a zombie. Where was my best self, I wondered?

Underneath Reliable Rob, where was Real Rob? The guy who cared about his wife and wanted to experience possibility and explore fulfillment and make a contribution and so much more?

I had to break free from the patterns of the past.

I was creating chaos for myself. Do you see it? Have you seen it in yourself?

If you want to change your world, or your organization, the journey always begins at the same place: inside. Teaching leadership without helping people to explore Self-leadership is a fool's errand. It's like putting racing wheels on a stagecoach. No matter how efficient those wheels might be, that stagecoach is never going to get on the freeway. Sure, you've got slick racing tires, and maybe you've got six or even 16 horses pulling that really efficient leadership stagecoach. But guess what? A stagecoach is never ever going to get you onto the freeway.

Coaching isn't about "faster tires." Coaching is about helping you to see the value in the way you are really designed. Bolt-on techniques won't make a difference if your protector parts keep blocking you from the redesign you really need. Believe me, I know.

My Self-leadership was toxic. I was dying on the inside. As an engineer, I realized the folly in trying to be someone I was not. There was a flaw in the design. Not in the way I was designed, but in the way I was taught to access leadership. Putting racing tires on a stagecoach? What kind of chaotic nonsense is that?

What if I weren't a stagecoach, trying to get onto the freeway? What if I were something more? What if the way I was designed was for a greater purpose? What would change?

The answer is: everything.

My friend, I am not magic. I am a guy from Canada who went through some really dark shit and came out the other side. And that's why I know—I KNOW—that you can, too. Because I know you have new possibilities inside of you.

Today, I live with my amazing wife and the world's greatest labradoodle in Costa Rica. We've added a new girl to the mix, and her name is Sasha—she's a high-energy Canaan dog. And our cat, Mowgli, now rules over all of us. We are in the mountains in the southern province of San José. We're about an hour inland from the beach. Up in the mountains, the weather is perfect.

I walk outside and I say, "Wow." I am surrounded by chaos, in the jungle, in the weather, in the thoughts inside of my head… and yet, I have capitalized on all of it. You can, too.

Coaching allowed me to formalize my experience and turn it into a professional service for companies and clients alike. Now, I create safe spaces where we explore creating the future from the now—from a place of compassion, peace, and strength, we create change from the inside out. I invite you to join me in that journey.

Coaching helped me to tap into the deeper Self. Helped me to get curious, so that I could ask this question: Do I want to show up as a boss today? That wasn't a question about my job title, or a question of me stepping into a persona. I wasn't interested in putting on a different mask or drinking a bucket of bravado. I was done administering poison to myself. I was ready for the antidote. I was ready for authenticity.

Inside a powerful session, my coach told me I was a leader.

Who, me?

My parts couldn't believe it.

When the noise died down, and I found some calm and some space, I recognized the lies I had been telling myself. The self-inflicted wounds needed to stop.

I came to understand that I was absolutely the leader of myself. I was able to make choices and decisions and follow up with actions and hold myself accountable and even encourage myself when things got tough. My coach wasn't trying to flatter me or bullshit me into believing the prettiest lie she could think of. She was just telling me the truth.

She was holding up a mirror to my soul and reminding me who I really was. Unlike Reliable Rob, there was no mask—and that was what made her words 100% reliable.

A LEADER EMERGES

I decided to be the leader that I needed.

"Huh," I wondered to myself, "what if I'm not whale shit? What if I'm the thinker, not the thought? Maybe my coach is way off base, but what if she's not?"

I evaluated her words like an engineer might test a circuit: If I am a leader, I am capable of Self-leadership, right? Let's test that theory.

Good leadership wasn't what I had experienced in my organization.

How could I be good to myself when others had shared various versions of the Destructive Six with me?

That's when I realized: we can give to ourselves what we have not received.

That's how compassion works. Generosity. Caring. True, I can't give you a new Lamborghini if I don't have one to give. But I can encourage you, and care about you, even if that wasn't always what I experienced in my own career. And that's true for you, too.

Sometimes it is the people who have been denied the most who discover how to give. Isn't that interesting?

Leadership was a choice: I chose to not let the shortcomings of others keep me from who I was meant to be. Their scarcity (of wise direction, clear communication, and courage) pointed me towards an abundance of those things inside myself. I could choose differently. And so can you.

I decided to embrace my parts and come back to myself—and my values. As I left my corporate work and moved into coaching and running my own businesses, I realized something. A realization that led me to create these words that you are reading right now.

Working with thousands of leaders and aspiring leaders, I've come to see that the story of one of us can be the story of all of us. Underneath our differences, we discover what unites us.

We share the same humanity. The same resiliency. The same capacity for self-healing, and self-leadership.

From there, I was able to be the leader my clients need—helping them to co-create lives and opportunities and results that once seemed impossible.

Each day, I realize just how powerful our minds are when we point them in the right direction!

Come back to your Self.

Meet yourself again, for the first time.

See your experiences and your dreams with compassion and curiosity.

Embrace your values, your parts, and your past. Move away from fear and towards the Wow.

Give yourself permission to take the first step.

As Wayne Dyer said, "The more we give away, the more is given to us."

When you give yourself permission, you move away from chaos and towards your Self. That's the kind of Self-leadership that everyone—and every organization—can embrace.

What are you waiting for?

—Rob Kalwarowsky

SOURCES

American Psychological Association. (2024, May). *Violence against educators post-pandemic*. https://www.apa.org/news/press/releases/2024/05/violence-against-educators-post-pandemic

Amazon. (n.d.). *No Bad Parts: Restoring Wholeness*. https://www.amazon.com/No-Bad-Parts-Restoring-Wholeness/dp/1683646681/

College of Surgeons. (2024, October). *Violence escalates against surgeons and other healthcare workers*. https://www.facs.org/for-medical-professionals/news-publications/news-and-articles/bulletin/2024/october-2024-volume-109-issue-9/violence-escalates-against-surgeons-and-other-healthcare-workers/

Forbes. (2021, August 25). *Battling burnout, anxiety and building productivity: Do you need coaching or therapy?* https://www.forbes.com/sites/chriswestfall/2021/08/25/battling-burnout-anxiety-and-building-productivity-do-you-need-coaching-or-therapy/

Gallup. (n.d.). *Workplace challenges 2025*. https://www.gallup.com/workplace/654329/workplace-challenges-2025.aspx

Harvard Business Review. (2020, January). *To be a great leader, you need the right mindset*. https://hbr.org/2020/01/to-be-a-great-leader-you-need-the-right-mindset

LinkedIn News. (2024, October). *Overwhelmed by workplace change*. https://news.linkedin.com/2024/October/overwhelmed-by-workplace-change

MIT Sloan Management Review. (n.d.). *Toxic culture is driving the great resignation*. https://sloanreview.mit.edu/article/toxic-culture-is-driving-the-great-resignation/

National Nurses United. (2024, February). *Workplace violence survey report*. https://www.nationalnursesunited.org/sites/default/files/nnu/documents/0224_Workplace_Violence_Report.pdf

National Library of Medicine. (2009). *Workplace violence in the health sector*. https://www.ncbi.nlm.nih.gov/pmc/articles/PMC2652990

Wåhlin-Jacobsen, C., et al. (2021). *Appetite for destruction: Six types of destructive leadership*. *Frontiers in Psychology, 12*, 668838. https://www.frontiersin.org/journals/psychology/articles/10.3389/fpsyg.2021.668838/full

BBC. (2018, May 2). *How your workplace is killing you*. https://www.bbc.com/worklife/article/20180502-how-your-workplace-is-killing-you

Forbes Health. (n.d.). *What is Internal Family Systems therapy (IFS)?* https://www.forbes.com/health/mind/what-is-internal-family-systems-therapy-ifs/

Harvard Health Publishing. (n.d.). *Understanding the stress response*. https://www.health.harvard.edu/staying-healthy/understanding-the-stress-response

MIT Sloan Management Review. (n.d.). *Toxic culture is driving the great resignation*. https://sloanreview.mit.edu/article/toxic-culture-is-driving-the-great-resignation/

Neuroscience News. (2021, May 11). *Toxic workplaces increase risk of depression by 300%*. https://neurosciencenews.com/toxic-workplaces-depression-18790/

Northwestern Medicine. (n.d.). *5 things you never knew about fear*. https://www.nm.org/healthbeat/healthy-tips/emotional-health/5-things-you-never-knew-about-fear

Pfeffer, J. (n.d.). *The relationship between workplace stressors and health costs*. Stanford Graduate School of Business. https://www.gsb.stanford.edu/faculty-research/publications/relationship-between-workplace-stressors-mortality-health-costs-united

Psychology Today. (2020, August). *4 signs that a boss has a passive-aggressive leadership style*. https://www.psychologytoday.com/us/blog/the-mysteries-of-love/202008/4-signs-that-a-boss-has-a-passive-aggressive-leadership-style

Psychology Today. (2023, January). *Utterly silent: The passive-aggressive boss*. https://www.psychologytoday.com/us/blog/transforming-toxic-leaders/202301/utterly-silent-the-passive-aggressive-boss

Variety. (2016, August 12). *Thomas Gibson's 'Criminal Minds' firing: Previous incidents revealed*. https://variety.com/2016/tv/news/thomas-gibson-criminal-minds-firing-previous-incidents-1201836799/

YouTube. (n.d.). *Video: Jocko Willink // Embrace the SUCK *. https://youtu.be/GB18Y78l28o?si=HipLtdKs7e4WxyDy

Amazon. (n.d.). *Getting along: How to work with anyone (even difficult people)*. https://www.amazon.com/Getting-Along-Anyone-Difficult-People/dp/1647821061/

Amazon. (n.d.). *Should I stay or should I go: Surviving a relationship with a narcissist*. https://www.amazon.com/Should-Stay-Surviving-Narcissistic-Relationship/dp/1618688782

Forbes. (2019, October 27). *Senior executives are more likely to be psychopaths*. https://www.forbes.com/sites/stephaniesarkis/2019/10/27/senior-executives-are-more-likely-to-be-psychopaths/

Harvard Business Review. (2005, October). *The passive-aggressive organization*. https://hbr.org/2005/10/the-passive-aggressive-organization

Lewis Howes. (n.d.). *How to create boundaries with a narcissist* [Podcast episode]. https://lewishowes.com/podcast/how-to-create-boundaries-with-a-narcissist/

Lewis Howes. (n.d.). *Narcissists vs. psychopaths: How to avoid dating one with Dr. Ramani Durvasula – Part 1* [Podcast episode]. https://lewishowes.com/podcast/narcissists-vs-psychopaths-how-to-avoid-dating-one-with-dr-ramani-durvasula-part-1/

Mayo Clinic. (n.d.). *Sepsis - Symptoms and causes*. https://www.mayoclinic.org/diseases-conditions/sepsis/symptoms-causes/syc-20351214

Psychology Today. (2015, September). *Narcissist or just self-centered? 4 ways to tell*. https://www.psychologytoday.com/us/blog/fixing-families/201509/narcissist-or-just-self-centered-4-ways-tell

Psychology Today. (2023, January). *The hidden danger of the homicidal narcissist*. https://www.psychologytoday.com/us/blog/the-human-equation/202301/the-hidden-danger-of-the-homicidal-narcissist

Psychology Today. (n.d.). *Fantasies*. https://www.psychologytoday.com/us/basics/fantasies

Psychology Today. (n.d.). *Jealousy*. https://www.psychologytoday.com/us/basics/jealousy

Psychology Today. (n.d.). *Attention*. https://www.psychologytoday.com/us/basics/attention

Radical Candor. (n.d.). *Our approach*. https://www.radicalcandor.com/our-approach/

ScienceDirect. (n.d.). *Personality and Individual Differences: Article on psychopathy and leadership*. https://www.sciencedirect.com/science/article/abs/pii/S0191886915300830

University of Texas Medical Branch. (n.d.). *UTMB Impact article on workplace behavior*. https://www.utmb.edu/impact-archive/archive/article.aspx?IAID=1182

Warner Bros. Discovery. (2024). *Max Original comedy special: Hannah Einbinder – Everything Must Go*. https://press.wbd.com/us/na/media-release/max/max-original-comedy-special-hannah-einbinder-everything-must-go-debuts-june-13

Levin & Perconti. (n.d.). *Stages of sepsis*. https://www.levinperconti.com/nursing-home-abuse/sepsis/stages/

Choosing Therapy. (n.d.). *Can a narcissist change?* https://www.choosingtherapy.com/can-a-narcissist-change/

Quest for Meaning. (n.d.). *Violence never solves anything*. https://www.questformeaning.org/tag/violence-never-solves-anything/

YouTube. (n.d.). *Video: 4 Types of Narcissism*. https://youtu.be/_uJs0iGQN0M?si=jTLgMnfN_4Aorvb0

YouTube. (n.d.). *Video: How to Work with a Passive-Aggressive Coworker | The Harvard Business Review Guide*. https://youtu.be/-W4_I4nX2uI?si=4t4U0wA8TOG7IV2Q

YouTube. (n.d.). *Video: Antifragility: How to use suffering to get stronger | Jonathan Haidt & more*. https://youtu.be/ISjRSek5Xbs?si=kQhkLVJOPlXQ1o31

Greenleaf Center for Servant Leadership. (n.d.). *What is servant leadership?* https://www.greenleaf.org/what-is-servant-leadership/

Mangia, K. (n.d.). *Success from anywhere*. https://www.readsuccessfromanywhere.com/

Harvard Business Review. (2015, April). *How to respond when someone takes credit for your work*. https://hbr.org/2015/04/how-to-respond-when-someone-takes-credit-for-your-work

Bronee, J. (n.d.). *Official website of Jeanette Bronee*. https://www
.jeanettebronee.com/

Cunic, A. (2023, April 7). *What is the spotlight effect?* Verywell
Mind. https://www.verywellmind.com/what-is-the-spotlight
-effect-3024470

Dalhousie University. (n.d.). *David Lovas, MD – Faculty Profile*. https://
medicine.dal.ca/departments/department-sites/psychiatry/our
-people/faculty/david-lovas.html

Katie, B. (2017, October). *Four liberating questions*. The Work. https://
thework.com/2017/10/four-liberating-questions/

Psychology Today. (2022, June). *All eyes on us: The spotlight
effect*. https://www.psychologytoday.com/us/blog/parenting
-neuroscience-perspective/202206/all-eyes-us-the-spotlight-effect

YouTube. (n.d.). *Video: #54: "Don't Be The Cowardly Manager" | At the
Table with Patrick Lencioni *. https://youtu.be/uhDCDmjPBd0?si
=HBFqSW-IPJ0SdgbL

McGonigal, K. (2016). *The upside of stress: Why stress is good for
you, and how to get good at it*. Avery. https://www.amazon.com/
Upside-Stress-Why-Good-You/dp/1101982934

Shaheen, K. (n.d.). *The Shadow Work Journal: A guide to integrate and
transcend your shadows*. https://www.amazon.com/Shadow
-Work-Journal-Integrate-Transcend/dp/B09KN2QCML

Sherman, D. K., & Cohen, G. L. (2006). Psychology of self-defense:
Self-affirmation theory. *Advances in Experimental Social
Psychology, 38*, 183–242. https://core.ac.uk/download/pdf/
191843342.pdf

ABOUT THE AUTHOR

MIT alum. NCAA athlete. Engineer. High-performer in his native Canada. Rob Kalwarowsky had it all. So why was he on the verge of suicide? The chaos inside his organization was matched by an internal talk-track that was leaving him confused, frustrated and ready to end it all. But from depression came transformation: a powerful journey to self-leadership, acceptance and clarity that led beyond the toxic leadership and negative thinking that had stolen his focus. Confronting the personal and professional demons of chaos, Rob uncovered a proven way to help anyone (and any team) to enhance performance in the midst of uncertainty. By accessing new perspectives on self-leadership, his strategies help companies and high-growth business leaders to rise above the unpredictability of our times. A coach and TEDx keynote speaker, Rob capitalizes on chaos with multi-billion dollar international companies, entrepreneurs, executives and aspiring leaders. Find out more at www.robkalwarowsky.com

www.ingramcontent.com/pod-product-compliance
Lightning Source LLC
Chambersburg PA
CBHW030509210326
41597CB00013B/839